Limerick Boycott 1904

Anti-Semitism in Ireland

Limerick Boycott 1904

Anti-Semitism in Ireland

Dermot Keogh and Andrew McCarthy

MERCIER PRESS

Mercier Press
Douglas Village, Cork
Email: books@mercierpress.ie
Website: www.mercierpress.ie

Trade enquiries to CMD Distribution
55A Spruce Avenue, Stillorgan Industrial Park
Blackrock, County Dublin
Tel: (01) 294 2560; Fax: (01) 294 2564
E-mail: cmd@columba.ie

ISBN 185635 453 9
10 9 8 7 6 5 4 3 2 1

A CIP record for this title is available
from the British Library

Mercier Press receives financial assistance from
the Arts Council/An Chomhairle Ealaíon

Printed in Spain by GraphyCems

Contents

Preface

This book combines narrative with a large selection of contemporary documents from the files of the Chief Secretary's Office, Dublin Castle. The research for my *Jews in Twentieth Century Ireland* also forms the basis for this work.

What this work seeks to do is marry the narrative and select documents. It offers the reader the opportunity to review material from primary sources. This is the first in a series of studies the UCC Department of History hopes to produce for a general readership and for use in the teaching of history at secondary and third levels.

This book would not have been possible without the scholarship and the technological skills of my colleague, Dr Andrew McCarthy. His work provides a template for future volumes.

We are both very grateful to Aisling Lyons of Mercier Press who prepared the book for publication and to Clare Keogh for the cover design.

Our thanks also to Mary Feehan and other members of the Mercier staff who have supported the book.

We are grateful to the administrative staff of the History Department: Charlotte Holland, Margaret Clayton, Veronica Fraser, Geraldine McAlister, Deirdre O'Sullivan and Norma Buckley.

Thanks are also due to Vice-President Michael O'Sullivan of Cork University Press.

Mr Gerald Goldberg, who died last year, gave a number of interviews and was generous with his time and knowledge. His parents and extended family were victims of the Limerick boycott. Although he was not born until 1912, Gerald was a repository of historical information about Irish Jewish history and, in particular, about Limerick and his native Cork. We thank also Mr Fred Rosehill of the Cork Jewish community.

This book required extensive research in the National Archives Dublin. We thank its staff and, in particular, Catriona Crowe and Aideen Ireland.

We also thank Larry Walsh of Limerick Museum for kindly allowing us to reproduce some photographs.

The Redemptorist order in Limerick gave access to its community archives and its members challenged me to rethink a number of my original ideas during the course of a lively discussion in 2004.

My thanks also to Limerick diocesan archive.

The Irish Jewish Museum in Dublin is a memorial to the history, culture and traditions of the Jewish community over the past two hundred years. It is a museum, an archive and a convivial meeting place where staff are always willing to provide impromptu tours and share their considerable knowledge with visitors. We thank both the staff and the director of the museum, Raphael Siev, who has strong personal connections with Limerick. In 1904, his family owned a small shop in Limerick. It was attacked on the night of the first anti-Semitic sermon delivered by Fr Creagh in the Redemptorist Church.

This book is dedicated both to those who suffered in the attacks on the Jewish area of Limerick and also to those, like Michael Davitt, who spoke out at the time against anti-Semitism.

– Dr Dermot F. Keogh, MRIA
Head of Department of History, UCC
November 2004

Introduction

In January 1904 the head of Limerick city's Catholic arch-confraternity, Fr John Creagh, delivered a wide-ranging denunciation of Jews in history and their alleged contemporary business practices. The sermon was widely reported in the local and national newspapers. On the night it was delivered, there was an immediate backlash against the local Jewish community living around Colooney Street near the city centre.[1]

The violence was expressed in mob-like fashion as those attending Fr Creagh's evening sermon turned on the Jews when returning home. There followed a week of unrest with police deployed in the centre city area to protect the Jewish families. Creagh preached another sermon a week later in which he attempted to defend his words. His call for an economic boycott of Jewish traders and shops met with considerable success. This resulted in economic ruin for many of them, necessitating their departure from Limerick, to other Irish cities, and further afield. The Jewish community in Limerick declined after these events and never recovered.

These events have of course raised many questions, for historians, for social scientists, for religious people, and indeed for anyone with an interest in society and culture. Among the more common questions thrown up are the following: why did these events occur in Limerick, and only in Limerick? What actually happened there? How did people in general respond to the events? How in particular did people in authority, in government and the Catholic Church, respond to events? What role did the Royal Irish Constabulary play in meeting the unfolding situation? What role did the media – local and national – play in these events, and to what extent is the press coverage a reliable historical source for interpreting them? And the list generally goes on until the final really difficult question is asked: did the events in Limerick constitute a pogrom?

The objectives in compiling this document collection are partly to answer these questions, to bring the wider public closer to the events and, as far as possible, to let people judge the event for themselves through key documents.

There is a general narrative and interpretation of events offered in this book, based largely on the research and writing undertaken for *Jews in Twentieth Century Ireland* published in 1998.[2] That study examined the events in Limerick in detail, and recognised that Limerick stood out as an event of singular importance in the Jewish communities' historical experience in Ireland.

It was felt that to appreciate that experience, one really had to see the primary documentation itself, to feel history, and judge whether historians have been faithful to their sources and their overall discipline.

In this book, a wide range of documentation is laid out for the reader relating to events before and after January 1904 to place the event in proper historical perspective.

Of course, the documents published here represent only a fragment of the primary source material generated by the events. There are literally hundreds of pages: of published police notes, commentaries and recommendations, of observations of public officials, of private letters and correspondence of key individuals and outside third parties drawn into the dispute, and a weighty volume of media reports and published public letters in both local, national and British press.

But we believe the selection of documents here is representative of the overall collection. Inevitably, choices had to be made as to what should be included and omitted. The underlying rationale in making such choices was to try and reflect the weight of the material produced in the above areas and, when selecting a document, to consider the value of each piece to the particular section, and the overall work.

Certain decisions were also made in relation to interpretation of the documentation and it is as well to state these. Firstly, the contemporary media reports of Fr Creagh's speeches are accepted as accurate. Secondly, the police reports at local level are accepted as giving a fair account of events on the ground, insofar as they are generally fact-based. Thirdly, some of the subsequent media reporting, and numerous letters published in the press, is heavily slanted one way or the other – a fact that becomes apparent to the reader. This last point merely reflects the fact that as most controversies become publicised, the media is rarely a neutral bystander. And such would prove to be the case in the general reporting and attitudes expressed by the media in the case of Limerick.

Even before January 1904 the use and interpretation of language would have significant implications for the Jewish community in Ireland. In looking at the background to this one is struck by the manner in which language and innuendo intertwine in the Irish consciousness. A decade before the events in Limerick, rumour and insinuation put it about that the Jews in Ireland were engaged in nefarious business practices, selling recycled tea and other undesirable activities. Such rumours persisted to the point that in 1903 a nationwide, if discreet, police investigation of the activities of the Jewish community revealed all allegations to be unfounded. Rumour generally does not require foundation when the willingness to believe surpasses the demand for evidence. The market for accusations in Ireland was generally strong. Such a market shaped the working – and living – environment of the Jewish community for years. And in reality the exoneration of the 1903 investigation changed little: for how could a government announce it had just undertaken a covert investigation into the activities of a minority community, however favourable the results? Language and insinuation would remain just as powerful weapons after this event for that reason. In reality the Jewish community would continue to labour under a cloud of suspicion in certain quarters of the public mind. And when the people were openly encouraged by an authoritative figure to believe certain practices, habits and vices attributed to the Jewish community, the expected response would seem almost predictable.

The role of the police, or constabulary, is most interesting in the whole affair. In one small case study, one can see the whole apparatus of the police structure at work. And it was formidable. From discreetly instigating background searches on the whole of the Jewish communities' activities in 1903 to handling the issue locally in Limerick in 1904, the constabulary gave the impression of high competence and swift execution of duties.

Furthermore, particularly in the crucial period from January to March 1904, the local police as represented by District Inspector O'Hara played a defining role in how the events in Limerick played out. Local constabulary reports influenced the responses of superiors in the RIC and Dublin Castle, in terms of action to be taken on the ground, responding to Fr Creagh's actions, and affording protection for Jewish traders in Limerick city.

This 'bottom-up' policy formulation extended to Westminster where the Irish chief secretary, George Wyndham, responded along the lines recommended by his own officials, as influenced by the Limerick constabulary. The seemingly growing reliance on District Inspector O'Hara stemmed from the scrupulous intelligence reports he cabled to Dublin on a daily – sometimes twice-daily – basis.

One of the most intriguing questions of all is why these events in 1904 were only confined to Limerick. Why was it just a localised event? The answer to this question is neither simple nor singular: in reality a broad range of factors appears to have contributed to the uniqueness of Limerick.

From the earlier sections in this book it will be seen that the settlement patterns of the Jewish community in Ireland were replicated in most of the urban areas they settled: in Limerick, they concentrated around Colooney Street; in Cork they established 'Jewtown'; in Dublin they created 'little Jerusalem', and so forth in other large cities. And from the statistics on the growth of the community, we shall see that there was no disproportionate concentration of Jews in Limerick.

Nor was there anything exceptional in the occupations of Limerick's Jews: the majority of the community in Ireland were what might be termed petty traders of one sort or another, either sedentary or on the road. While we review the history of anti-semitism in Ireland in the earlier sections of the book, and find sporadic incidents over time, there does not appear to have been any previous sustained attack on them as a community, although granted further research may throw light on other parts of Ireland.

While the economic conditions of Limerick city were undoubtedly a major contributory factor, there is no doubt that similar conditions were replicated in practically every urban centre in the country at this time. Abject poverty, alcohol abuse and the ready market for the pawnbroker were not unique to Limerick.

What Limerick had in addition to all of these issues was a couple of factors that contributed to the timing of the event and possibly ensured it was contained in Limerick. In the person of Fr John Creagh they had a young and enthusiastic preacher. He came from a respected merchant family in Limerick – an avenue of investigation yet to be undertaken. He was head of the local arch-confraternity of the Holy Family. Founded on 20 January 1868 by the Redemptorists, an order of Italian origin, the arch-confraternity had about 6,000 members in 1904. The numbers were so large that it met in sections three nights a week. It recruited its support mainly, although not exclusively, from the poorer sectors of Limerick city and countryside. It was Fr Creagh's first speech to this body that started the controversy. Yet it is clear from the nature of the speech that it was well rehearsed, and obvious too that Fr Creagh was well prepared. He certainly had support for his ideas. He had a list compiled of judgements in Petty Sessions, etc.

During the controversy the local Rabbi Levin asked Michael Davitt to conclude for himself whether the anti-Semitic outburst had its roots in religious prejudices or had been promoted by local traders, suggesting that part of the blame lay with those members of the business community who felt threatened by the Jewish trade.

It was this combination of elements that ensured that it was only in Limerick – and mainly in Limerick city – that the economic boycott of the Jewish community prevailed.

A final vexatious question persists: did the events in Limerick constitute a 'pogrom'?

It is variously described in the literature of Limerick history as an economic boycott and a pogrom. Most recently, in his accomplished biography of Bishop Edward Thomas O'Dwyer of Limerick, the prolific Jesuit writer, Thomas Morrissey, introduces his section entitled 'The Jewish Boycott' but acknowledges in his conclusion that in the minds of Limerick's Jews, it was the 'Limerick Pogrom'.[3] But is the use of the latter term justified despite the fact that nobody was killed or seriously injured? Based on their experiences in Lithuania, the word 'pogrom' came immediately to the lips of Limerick's Jews when they found themselves under attack in January 1904.[4] Those fears must further be seen in the context of a country which was overwhelmingly Christian.

Ultimately, of course, it is for the reader to judge whether the events should be viewed as a boycott or a pogrom. If this documentary reader helps in forming that view, so much the better. The fact that we have chosen to entitle the book 'Limerick Boycott 1904' will indicate our preference, but nothing can detract from the terror experienced by the Jews of Limerick on the evening of Fr Creagh's first sermon.

– Dermot Keogh and Andrew McCarthy
November 2004

The Growth of the Jewish Community in Ireland

The majority of Jews who arrived in Ireland between 1800 and 1880 were Ashkenazi (Jews from northern or eastern Europe). Before 1800, the Sephardi (descendants of the Jews expelled from Spain in 1492), were better represented in the tiny Irish Jewish community.[5] Most of those who arrived up to the 1880s settled in Dublin where the community grew slowly, as reflected by the total of only 308 births recorded between 1838 and 1879.[6]

In Belfast, there are, according to Bernard Shillman, no records of Jews in the city before 1814.[7] But by 1891, there were 282 Jews in what is now Northern Ireland, with the majority, 205, living in Belfast.[8] Credit for the founding of the Belfast congregation went to Daniel Joseph Jaffe, whose son, Otto, was a distinguished businessman, governor of the Royal Hospital, German consul, and twice-elected lord mayor of Belfast.[9] Otto Jaffe was a life-president of the Belfast congregation and would be actively involved in supporting the Jewish community in Limerick in 1904.

According to the 1871 census there were 6 Jews living in Cork, the largest city in Munster. By 1881 there were 10 but that figure had risen to 155 by 1891 and to 359 by 1901. The new arrivals settled in the Eastville area, which quickly became known, without any pejorative overtones, as 'Jewtown'.[10] It was 'a Lithuanian village inserted in the midst of a very parochial people'. Those who settled in Cork were almost exclusively from the districts of Vilna and Kovno.[11] Most had been neighbours in the village of Akmijan and sought to be so again – in Cork.[12] They were later joined by Louis Goldberg and his young family, who, like many others, moved to Cork to escape the Limerick boycott in 1904.[13] Census returns record 1 Jew living in Limerick in 1861, 2 in 1871 and 4 in 1881, rising to 35 in 1888, to 90 in 1892, reaching 130 in 1896.

The real growth of the Jewish community in Ireland occurred after the Russian pogroms which followed the assassination of Tsar Alexander II by revolutionaries in March 1881.[14] Russia's anti-Semitic press blamed the Jews, triggering riots in southern Russia and into Poland.[15] Repressive legislation dating back to 1804 was strengthened by further anti-Semitic provisions in 1882 and again in 1891.[16] From 1880 to 1914, about two million Russian Jews emigrated, mostly to the USA, while some settled in Palestine, Canada, South Africa, Britain and Ireland.[17]

Many who settled in Ireland were from the province of Kovno Gubernia in Lithuania. The core of the Dublin and Cork communities came from 'a rather derelict place called Akmijan'.[18] According to Len Yodaiken, whose family settled in Dublin, 'in the old days, in Dublin, if you did not have an ancestor from Akmijan, you did not belong to the "Club"'.[19] Jewish immigrants also came from Zhager (today called Zagare), Klikul (Klykoliai), Vexna or Svexna, Papiljan, Kurshjan (Kursenai) and Shavli (Siaulia); between 1881 and 1901, hundreds fled to Ireland from Akmijan and these other

Year	Total S.I. Population	No. of Jews	% Increase or Decrease
1861	4,402,111	341	–
1871	4,053,187	230	-32.6
1881	3,870,020	394	+71.3
1891	3,468,694	1,506	+282.2
1901	3,221,823	3,006	+99.6
1911	3,139,688	3,805	+26.6
1926	2,971,992	3,686	-3.1
1936	2,968,420	3,749	+1.7
1946	2,955,107	3,907	+4.2

Lithuanian villages.[20] Among those who fled to Ireland were the Rosehill, Abrahamson, Briscoe, Goldberg, Good, Marcus, Nurock, Siev and Wine families – all of whom emerged as prominent in Ireland's Jewish community. The growth of the Jewish community in southern Ireland (now the Republic of Ireland) is reflected in the census returns shown above.

The distribution of the Jewish population, based on official readings of the 1891 and 1901 census returns, was as follows:

DOCUMENT 1B

*The Number
and Distribution
of the Jewish
Community in
Ireland,
1891–1901*

Source: CSORP,
1905/23538, NAI

Provinces and Counties	No. of Jews 1891	1901
Leinster		
Carlow County	5	9
Dublin City	971	2,048
Dublin County	86	121
Kildare County	15	8
Kilkenny County	1	2
Kilkenny City	11	–
King's County [Offaly]	6	9
Longford County	–	3
Louth Co. (incl. Drogheda)	7	54
Meath County	3	13
Queen's County [Laois]	9	3
Westmeath County	1	3
Wexford County	2	8
Wicklow County	18	15
Total of province	1,135	2,296
Munster		
Clare County	1	
Cork County	62	88
Cork City	155	359
Kerry County	13	8
Limerick County	–	–
Limerick City	93	171
Tipperary County	11	20
Waterford County	4	–
Waterford City	15	42
Total of province	354	688

Ulster

Antrim County	2	37
Armagh County	33	44
Belfast City	205	708
Cavan County	2	1
Donegal County	–	–
Down County	26	34
Fermanagh County	–	3
Londonderry City	5	58
Londonderry County	–	6
Monaghan County	7	6
Tyrone County	2	2
Total of province	282	899

Connaught

Galway County	–	1
Leitrim County	2	–
Mayo County	2	–
Roscommon County	1	–
Sligo County	3	14
Total of province	8	15

Total of Ireland	**1,779**	**3,898**

The Jewish Community
in Limerick

This influx of refugee Jews created for the first time Jewish quarters in the two largest cities, Dublin and Belfast, as well as in Limerick and Cork. About twenty-five families of Lithuanian Jews had settled in Limerick by 1900, mainly in the poor section around Edward Street.[21] Among these immigrants was Louis Goldberg, who moved to Cork following the 1904 boycott. The testimony of his son, Gerald (a former lord mayor of Cork and a distinguished solicitor), and the unpublished memoir of his daughter, Fanny (mother of the novelist, David Marcus), vividly portray the early years of the Jewish community in Limerick.[22] Because this story is so typical of the Jews who emigrated to Ireland, it is worth recalling the details as they provide a crucial historical background to events in 1904.

One of a large family, Louis Goldberg escaped conscription into the Russian army at the age of fourteen as the pogroms forced him to flee Akmijan in 1882. He travelled to Riga, where the authorities refused American emigration to a number of boys in his group. Possibly because of his fair colouring, he was allowed to proceed, finding passage on a timber ship sailing to Ireland – the supposed first leg of his journey to America. He had never seen a map until he came to Ireland and did not know the distance to America.

Put ashore at Queenstown (now Cobh), he had the

COLOONEY
STREET
RESIDENTS

*Albert Siev and
Edith Arnovitch
at their wedding
in Limerick in
1919. The Siev
family was to
emerge as
prominent in
Ireland's Jewish
community.*

Photograph courtesy of
Jewish Museum,
Dublin

good fortune to be met by another Lithuanian Jew, Isaac
Marcus, who regularly went to the docks to offer help to
newly arrived co-religionists. He was taken to the home
of the Sandlers, also from Akmijan. There Goldberg first

met Rachel, who became his wife in 1891; she had arrived in Cork with her family from Lithuania in 1875 as a one-year-old child. The Sandlers kindly allowed him to rest for a few days in their home, where he became familiar with members of the small but growing Jewish community in Cork, his lifelong friend Zalman Clein among them. Within weeks of his arrival Louis set out on foot for Dublin – a distance of 158 miles. There he met a co-religionist named Jackson, who loaned him ten shillings with which he purchased a pedlar's licence and a small stock of holy pictures of Roman Catholic saints and popes. He returned to Cork on foot, selling his merchandise on the way.

Having family friends from Akmijan in Limerick, Goldberg moved there in 1883 and was taken in by his relatives, the Greenfields. The Weinronks, who arrived from Akmijan in the 1870s, were also his cousins. The two families remained very close during their Limerick sojourn. Goldberg was most probably related on his father's side to the Barrons, another Jewish family in Limerick.

Louis Goldberg continued working as a pedlar, travelling in the city and around the countryside. His daughter, Fanny, born in 1893, recalled in her memoirs the harsh life of her father. She remembered seeing the pedlars walking through the streets of Limerick laden with their goods strapped on their shoulders and, sometimes, with picture frames hanging on their arms: 'Rain and cold didn't cry halt. They had their families to keep,' she stated. They were often known to their customers as 'tally men'. Working on the weekly payments system, the debt was marked down in a book and the 'tally' added up. With their broken English, the word 'weekly' became 'vickla';

in certain Jewish communities, vickla was the only word used to describe their business as 'tally men'. As they went about their work, Fanny recalled that children in the streets of Limerick used to run after the 'tally men', with their backs bent from their packs, shouting 'a pitchie [picture] man, a tally man, a Jew, Jew, Jew'. 'I wonder often how they lived,' she reminisced. The 'weeklies' also worked on foot in the countryside, returning to the cities at the weekend in time for the Sabbath.

Louis' son, Gerald, born in Cork in 1912, recalled that his father had been shown great kindness and hospitality by country women in County Clare. On one occasion Louis was invited into a cottage and offered a glass of milk by the woman of the house; being a strict orthodox Jew though he would not drink milk that he had not seen coming directly from the cow. And so he politely refused but offered instead to milk the cow, which enabled him to drink the milk. Befriended by the family, he was allowed to sleep in the house where – on other visits – he learned to sing lullabies in Irish which he later sang to his own children. It was, however, more usual for Louis to sleep in an outhouse while on the road. His was the common lot of the Jewish pedlar – a frequent sight in turn-of-the-century Ireland.

When prosperous enough in the mid-1880s, Louis rented a house in Mount Pleasant Avenue, off Colooney Street, in Limerick. He brought his mother over from Russia; Bubba (grandmother) Elka became a very strong force in his life, in that of his future family and in the life of the community. Louis travelled to Cork regularly to buy stock for his business, and he frequently visited the home of the Sandlers at 13 Elizabeth Terrace, Cork.

One day he saw a beautiful young woman scrubbing the wooden kitchen floor; it was Rachel, the girl he had first seen as an eight-year-old child when he had landed in Ireland in 1882. He was introduced to her by her mother. He was so impressed that he immediately visited an old friend from Akmijan, Zalman Clein, and told him that he wanted to marry the girl. He asked Clein to make the match. She was seventeen and he was twenty-four. Never allowed to 'walk out' together, the couple were married on 18 September 1891 at the *shul*, or synagogue, in 24 South Terrace, Cork. They went to live in Limerick at 50 Coloney Street, next door to Coll's public house; they ran a small grocery shop from the house and Louis continued to travel as a pedlar.

Later in the decade, the family moved to 47 Henry Street, where Louis had a small drapery store. While the business did not provide the family with a luxurious standard of living, Bubba Elka was a strong woman known for her beautiful baking and her capacity to improvise. When, for example, kosher wine was not to be found in Limerick, she made it for special religious festivals. Rachel's mother also travelled from Cork, sometimes with her younger children, to help look after the household when her daughter had a child. By 1901, she had two daughters, Fanny (b. 1893) and Molly (b. 1896) and one son, Henry (b. 1899). She had another boy in 1904. In all, Rachel had thirteen children who lived. Rachel's brother, Joseph Sandler, also lived with the family for a time, as did Louis' youngest brother, Solomon or Sol, later a significant figure in the Zionist movement. Thanks to Louis' financial help, his two other brothers, Bernard and Samuel, had also come to

LIMERICK
SHOP FRONT

*The shop was
owned by the
Siev family in the
1880s.*

Photograph courtesy
of the Jewish
Museum, Dublin

live in Limerick by the turn of the century. Samuel lived
at 15 Emmet Place with his wife, Rachel, and their two
sons and two daughters; Bernard lived at 9 Colooney
Street with his wife, Sima, and their three daughters and
three sons. Their cousins, the Weinronks, lived nearby.
According to the 1901 census, Bernard Weinronk lived
at 27 Bowman Street with his wife, Sarah, and daughter,
Jennette. David Weinronk lived at 46 Colooney Street
with his wife, Sophia, daughter, Hanna, aged twenty and
son, Simon, aged eighteen.

The 1901 census provides details of the many other
Jewish families who had settled in Limerick by this time
(see Appendix for full listing). It is noteworthy that,
with the exception of the Jaffes, where there was a dentist and a dental mechanic in the family, and William
Marcus Stein, who was also a dental mechanic, most

Jews in Limerick were pedlars. A small minority described themselves as drapery dealers and grocers. All the Jewish grocery shops were near to one another in Colooney Street, at the end near to the main street. Practically all the Jewish homes in Limerick listed in the 1901 census had a Roman Catholic servant. This did not reflect exalted status but it showed that by 1901 many Jewish families were not to be ranked as being at the lowest end of the social ladder.

The first place of prayer the Limerick Jewish community had was a private house in Emmet Place. The congregation then moved to 18 Colooney Street. A more permanent place of worship was found at No. 63. But a schism over interpretations of observance of the law quickly divided the small community, and two rival houses of prayer emerged in the 1890s. Personal conflicts, which had sometimes ended in litigation, further complicated intra-community relations. The issue of moneylending was, according to the Limerick historian, Des Ryan, also a source of conflict within the community and had been condemned by the chief rabbi of the United Kingdom, Dr Hermann Adler, on two visits to the city in 1892 and 1898. Louis Goldberg first opened a rival synagogue in his Henry Street home. The synagogue was moved to 72 Colooney Street in 1901. (Rabbi Levin's synagogue was at No. 63.) Letters from the rival groups appeared in the *Limerick Leader*. M. J. Blond wrote in January 1901 that the only authorised synagogue was at 63 Colooney Street and that in the minds of 'our Christian neighbours and friends' the rival was a 'so-called Synagogue', he wrote. Goldberg replied that 'the principal reason for establishing the [new synagogue] is not to associate ourselves

FREEDMAN'S
GROCERY STORE

The store was run by Colooney Street residents Malka and Art Freedman.

Photograph courtesy of
the Jewish Museum,
Dublin

with moneylenders, and these are the full wishes of our Chief Rabbi, Rev. Dr Adler'. The Goldberg group had the support of about ten families, the oldest families in the city who, according to Louis, had 'built up the Jewish congregation, and this is not the first time in our Jewish history that our Tribe has had to make room for some upstarts. History repeats itself.'[23] The divisions within the Limerick Jewish community were, as the above demonstrates, highly personalised and acrimonious.

Anti-Semitism in Ireland

During a visit to Ireland in 1892 to consecrate the new headquarters of the Dublin Hebrew Congregation at Adelaide Road,[24] Rev. Dr S. Hermann Adler, the chief rabbi of the British empire, told the congregation: 'You have come here, my foreign brethren, from a country like unto Egypt of old to a land which offers you hospitable shelter. It is said that Ireland is the only country in the world which cannot be charged with persecuting the Jews.'[25] Rabbi Adler was generous in his remarks. The Irish administration in the nineteenth century did not persecute Jews. But Jews in Ireland, and the 'new' Jews in particular, did have to confront incidents of anti-Semitism.

On Easter Sunday 1884 a crowd surrounded the house of Lieb Siev in Limerick, and stones were thrown, injuring Siev's wife and child.[26] Two ringleaders were sentenced to a month in prison with hard labour. Limerick's mayor, Alderman Lenihan, stated at the trial that the treatment of the Sievs could not be tolerated in a civilised country. *The Cork Examiner* warned: 'This country has long been honourably distinguished by its tolerance towards the Jews … *Haud Ignora Mali* – not ignorant of persecution and its evils, our own race ought to be especially careful to avoid its infliction.'[27] Nevertheless, two Jews were beaten up in the city in 1892, and in another incident, the house of Moses Leone was stoned on 24 November 1896.[28]

In Cork in 1888, two 'foreigners' known as Katz

threatened to import both cheap labour and cheap produce from abroad. The two were popularly believed to be Jews, although this has not been verified. Threats were made against the Jewish community by a number of trade unionists. The mayor of Cork, John O'Brien, wrote a letter to the London Times dissociating the city's population from these threats.[29] Again, there were indiscriminate attacks on Jews in Cork in 1894, with three of those responsible imprisoned.[30] The leader of the Irish Parliamentary Party, John Redmond, said on 9 May 1894 that he had 'no sympathy with the persecution to which the Jewish community have been subjected in other countries'. He felt sure that 'the great body of Catholics in Ireland who have in the past known what persecution for religion's sake meant, will never have any sympathy with the attacks upon the members of any creed'.[31]

In Dublin in 1886, there was an anti-Semitic poster campaign, supported by letters to newspapers, against the newly arrived Jews. Rallying to their defence, the Freeman's Journal wrote: 'This sudden antipathy to the Jewish community in the city is either the work of some hare-brained, or, what is more likely, the project of a set of ruffians having some ulterior object in view.'[32] Chief Rabbi Adler complained to Archbishop William Walsh of Dublin in October of that year:

> When I paid a Pastoral visit some years ago to the Hebrew Congregation of Dublin I made mention of the fact, which was afterwards published throughout the land, that Ireland was the only European country in which the Jews have never been persecuted. I have now learnt, with keen regret, that some evil disposed persons or person in your city have published placards casting reflections upon my

co-religionists residing in Dublin and inciting to their persecution and expulsion. I am convinced that your Grace
cannot approve of any members of the Irish people joining
in that anti-Semitic movement which has been disgracing
other countries, and I would appeal to your Grace to use
your powerful influence to stamp out the movement, ere,
God forfend, it should assume larger and more mischievous proportions.

I beg to assure your Grace of my sincere gratitude for
any measures you may deem fit in your wisdom to take in
this cause, and have the honor to remain.[33]

Archbishop Walsh then responded positively as Adler
later expressed his 'appreciation of the promise you are
good enough to make that should occasion arise – Heaven
forbid – you will devote your powerful influence to the
protection of my brethren in Dublin'.[34]

On 13 July 1893 – less than a year after Chief Rabbi
Adler's laudatory sermon – the Land League leader,
Michael Davitt, reproached Labour Federation representative, Con Crowley, who suggested that 'the Jews ought
to be kept out of Ireland'.[35] Davitt, who often defended
Irish and Russian Jews, wrote to the *Freeman's Journal*:
'The Jews have never to my knowledge done any injury
to Ireland', and exhorted the Irish to maintain their
proud record of tolerance.[36] He recalled the 1787 Irish
House of Commons resolution for the naturalisation of
all Jews who wished to become Irish citizens. Davitt also
advised the Irish against sympathising with anti-Semitic
campaigns in working-class London, where Tory protec-
tionists alleged that trade depression was traceable to
the influx of 'foreign workmen, mainly Jews'. As Irish
men and women were scattered the world over, Davitt
proclaimed:

... we are bound in justice and in reason to extend to all who seek the shelter of our island shores the same treatment and hospitality which the members of our own race have received at the hands of so many nations all over the globe, when driven by persecution and unjust government from their own country.[37]

Fr Thomas Finlay, SJ, responded with an editorial in the *Lyceum*, a magazine associated with the Catholic University.[38] He advised the native Irish to adopt measures of self-defence, though not of persecution, against immigrants whose settlement in the country would constitute an economic danger:

Our first duty is to ourselves and to our own people, and no sympathy with the suffering and persecuted Jews can avail to free us from this obligation. If the influx of the Jews into Ireland constitutes an economic danger to the industry of the wealth-producing classes amongst us, then it would be a duty to resist – not out of hatred of the Jews, but out of concern for ourselves.[39]

Finlay further warned that:

In Dublin, where they are settling in ever increasing numbers, they do not gravitate towards the Coombe or the Liberties. They possess themselves rather of the quarter traversed by the South Circular Road. In this thoroughfare itself and in the streets opening off they have established a flourishing colony – so flourishing that for their religious needs a spacious synagogue has lately been built close by. In some of the streets that open off the South Circular Road one may walk along the pavement from end to end and hardly hear a word of English spoken by the children who are at play on the footpath. We are in as completely a Jewish quarter as if we were wandering through some city of Poland or Southern Russia. But tenants of the houses which line the street are not of the social standing of the inhabitants of the Polish ghetto, nor are they given to the occupations of the 'sweated' Jew of London. They are respectable in their way, well dressed and well fed, not at all likely to compete with our poor tradesmen for the 'jobs' on which they depend for a livelihood.[40]

He attributed the election of a number of anti-Semitic candidates to the German parliament as evidence of their dislike of Jews, which arose 'from the fact that the Jew amongst them is a gombeen man' and that he contrives 'by tricks of trade and the devices of the moneylender' to get control of 'the wealth that the toiling Christian creates'. Finlay claimed that the Jew became 'a hawker and trader first, then a moneylender, and, finally a lord of the Money Market and Stock Exchange where he holds the destinies of nations in his hands'.[41] Therefore the 'danger' to Irish social and economic life came from the Jew's 'gombeening propensities'.

> We may notice him traversing the lanes of our cities, or visiting our country farm-houses when the 'good man' is abroad and only the woman of the household has to be dealt with. He carries bundles of cheap wares, or he is laden with pious pictures, or statues of the Christian Redeemer whose name and whose following he abhors. ... The Jew will be content to take his payment in weekly instalments. ... The 'Jewman' of Dublin, like the 'tickman' of Belfast, is an acknowledged acquaintance of the households with which he traffics and from which he collects his weekly contributions; it becomes easy for him to determine who are the 'good men' in his sphere of business, that is to say, in the Shylock's sense of the words, who are 'sufficient'.[42]

The editorial pointed out that the arrival of the Jew in Ireland as a trader coincided with a change in the law which gave the Irish tenant farmer a saleable interest in his farm, but trusted that 'it was no more than coincidence'. Nevertheless, Finaly speculated on what Jews were doing driving along country roads 'in smart vehicles, making calls at the houses of some of the farmers as they go', without the familiar pack and without Christian pictures and statues: 'Their visits are not undertaken out of friendship or philanthropy. What then?'[43] The implication was that the newly arrived Jews were intent on taking over Irish farms.

Having laid out those arguments, the editorial asked whether the Jew should be made welcome in Ireland. The answer was a qualified 'yes'. There ought to be a welcome if the Jew was to become an honest producer. But if he came merely 'as a parasite, not to produce by labour in the field or the workshop' but to live upon the fruits of the labours of others, then 'let him not be more welcome here than he is among the peasants of Germany or among the labourers of France'.[44]

*

The fears generated by the new arrivals in Ireland were exacerbated by growing anti-Semitism on the continent. The case of Alfred Dreyfus, a captain in the French army who had been convicted of spying for Germany and was sentenced on 22 December 1894 to imprisonment on Devil's Island, divided Irish society.[45] Furthermore, the clash between church and state in France also had an impact on opinion in Ireland.[46] There was no publication in Ireland to rival *La Croix*, a Catholic daily paper edited by Fr Bailly for the Assumptionist order which was proud to call itself 'the most anti-Semitic paper in France',[47] or the even more extreme anti-Semitism that could be found in the writings of Edouard Adolphe Drumont and his paper, *La Libre Parole*.[48] Nevertheless, the founder of the Sinn Féin movement, Arthur Griffith, while no Drumont, allowed anti-Semitic views to be published in his newspaper, the *United Irishman*.[49] In late 1899, Griffith wrote in the *United Irishman*: 'I have in former years often declared that the Three Evil Influences of the century were the Pirate, the Freemason, and the Jew.'[50] Griffith, who had lived in South Africa, wrote of the 'swarming Jews of Johannesburg', and of a 'sorry gathering' in Hyde Park:

> Some thirty thousand Jews and Jewesses, mostly of phenomenal ugliness and dirt, had come out of their East End dens at the summons of their Rabbis. If they hated France, it was also evident that they detested soap and water still more acutely. It was a scene to recall Thackeray's
>
> > All the fleas in Jewry
> > Jumped up and
> > bit like fury.[51]

The Dreyfus case was taken up again by *La Croix* in France[52] and by the *United Irishman*.[53] The latter paper showed no sympathy whatsoever for Dreyfus, and, following the quashing of his guilty verdict and the ordering of a retrial on 3 June 1899, the *United Irishman* argued on 5 August:

> While the Dublin Editors have fed the Irish public on the fables of the Jew Telegram Agencies, every diplomatist in Europe knows why [General Gaston] Galliffet [chosen to

review the guilty verdict in the Dreyfus case] has been chosen to be the Tool of the Jews at the French War Office. He has been for many years their servile debtor, absolutely living on their loans, and only able to pay as interest his 'aristocratic service' in getting rich Jews into 'good society'.[54]

Dreyfus was retried and condemned on 9 September but 'with extenuating circumstances'.[55] An article in an unrepentant *United Irishman* stated on 16 September:

A few days ago a Jew traitor, who had sold the most vital secrets of France to her military enemies, was condemned to the mild punishment of imprisonment, after his guilt had been for a second time in five years demonstrated to a court martial of his comrades ... The simple fact is that the whole European world, with the exception of the Anglo-Jew coalition and its Irish sycophants, is utterly indifferent to the traitor's fate.[56]

Dreyfus was pardoned by presidential decree on 19 September 1899 and completely exonerated by the French government on 12 July 1906. The radical socialist, Frederick Ryan, spoke for many of his contemporaries when he wrote in a letter to the *United Irishman* on 26 August 1899:

What do you think [Wolfe] Tone would have thought could he have seen a paper, allied with his memory, filling its columns with 'anti-Semitic' ravings – Tone, who was above all bigotries, and whose conspicuous service was to work for the emancipation of those of a faith [different] to that in which he himself was reared?[57]

Whether Finlay's allegations in the *Lyceum* reflected or

influenced opinion is not known for certain. What is clear, however, is that similar suggestions regarding Jewish activities still circulated at the turn of century, prompting Dublin Castle to investigate. In February 1903 the under secretary, Sir Antony MacDonnell, requested the chief commissioner of the Dublin Metropolitan Police, Sir John Ross, to make inquiries regarding the Jewish community (see document 2). A similar request was made of the inspector general of the Royal Irish Constabulary, Colonel Neville F. F. Chamberlain, regarding the whole country.

Specific inquiries were made regarding the position in Limerick:

> RIC Office
> Dublin Castle
> 4 February 1903

Co. Inspector of Limerick

With reference to my graph minute of 30th ultimo, it has been stated that Jew pedlars are getting the peasantry into debt in many places.

It is also asserted that some Jews are in the habit of collecting from hotels and other large establishments used tea leaves, drying them, mixing them with drugs and selling this compound to the poor people as tea.

Please make careful inquiry as to any Jew tea-dealer in your County, if there is any reason to be true. If tea is sold by travelling Jews is it possible to obtain sample packets of it for purposes of analysis?

District Inspector C. H. O'Hara, who was based in Limerick city and played a prominent role in investigating

Chief Commissioner,

D. M. Police.

It is observed from the Census
Returns that there has been, during
the decade 1891-1901, a considerable
increase in the number of Jews in
Ireland and particularly in Dublin
City.   The number of Jews in Dublin
in 1891 was 971, and the number in
1901 was 2,048.

Will you kindly report, for the
information of Government, whether
the increase has continued - and if
so to what extent - since 1901; what
are the causes of such increase; and,
specially, whether there is reason to
believe that the Jews are in any cases
endeavouring to get farmers into their
hands with a view to the acquisition
of land.

It has been stated that Jews are
in the habit of collecting from hotels,
and other large establishments of the
sort, used tea leaves, ~~dyeing~~ *drying* them,
mixing with them deleterious drugs,
and selling the compound to the poorer
classes as tea; and it has been suggested that this product must be injurious
to health, even producing nervous

disease and insanity.   Will you
kindly ascertain whether there is
any foundation in fact for this
suggestion.

2nd February 1903.

DOCUMENT 2
1903 LETTER TO
SIR JOHN ROSS

*Sir Antony
MacDonnell
requests that
Sir John Ross
make enquiries
regarding the
Jewish
community*

23

the assaults on Jews in 1904, reported in February 1903 that the allegations in relation to the Jews were unfounded in Limerick (document 3).

In addition, the county inspectors' reports for the rest of the country suggest the allegations about Jewish activities were totally unfounded. Having received the reports, Inspector General Chamberlain advised Under Secretary MacDonnell that there was 'no reason at present to believe that Jews are obtaining any hold on farms' (see document 4). Chamberlain told MacDonnell that, without exception, the county inspectors' reports (see document 5) supported the conclusion that 'there is no reason to believe that Jew tea Pedlars are in the habit of selling deleterious tea'.[58]

In the case of moneylending, police enquiries turned up seven cases – four in Cork and one each in Laois, Louth and Waterford – where Jews secured court judgments during 1902 against farmers. In none of the cases did the moneylenders, all with offices in Dublin (Liebe Levin, Joseph Levin in four of the cases and William Allaun in two), obtain any hold on the farms of their debtors. Despite being exonerated in the eyes of the police, suspicions lingered over alleged Jewish exploitation of poorer sections of the community.[59]

I beg report

I There is a slight decrease in the number of Jews in the city of Limerick since 1901

II They are chiefly pedlars & small shopkeepers. A few of them control a Loan Fund society. None of them hold land.

III They do not lend money to a very great extent to tenant farmers, but a good many small farmers & labourers in the rural part of this district are in debt to them for goods sold & delivered or, in a few cases, for money lent.

I do not think that their object is to obtain mortgages on the land.

As a rule they do not allow the debts to run to a large amount.

C. H. O'Hara
D.I.

Limerick 13: 2: 1903

Submitted the Jews all reside in the city & though they trade through the County among poor people. I cannot find that they try to interfere with the farmers Nor can I find that they lend money for the purpose of getting possession of the farms. I have made personal inquiry in several parts of the

County with the above result — which is same as reported [...]

Limerick 5. 11. 1903
To the D I at Limerick

T. Hayes C.I.

The D I /
Limerick
Limerick 12. 2. 3

The Jew pedlars have not got the peasants in the rural portion of this district into their debt to any great extent.

They do not sell tea here; nor do they buy used tea leaves at hotels or other places. Enquiries have been made at the large drapery houses, hotels, &c. & used tea leaves are not sold.

Mr. Hugh Coyle, George St., sends out a number of agents about the country & samples of the tea sold by them can be obtained.

C. H. O'Hara
D I

C.I.

DOCUMENT 3
FEBRUARY 1903
O'HARA'S
REPORT

District Inspector
C. H. O'Hara
wrote this report
at the behest of
County Inspector
Thomas Hayes

Under Secretary

DOCUMENT 4
FEBRUARY 1903
LETTER TO
UNDER
SECRETARY
MACDONNELL
FROM DUBLIN
CASTLE

Chamberlain
supported reports
that allegations
about the Jews
were unfounded

I submit reports from all the County Inspec-
tors in Ireland in reply to a Circular which I issued asking
certain questions as to the Jews now residing and trading
in the Country.

You will see from a copy of this Circular, annexed at
back, that I asked three distinct questions:-

I. As to any increase in the No. of Jews.

II. As to their occupation.

III. As to their dealings with farmers.

I annex a brief summary of the County Inspectors reports
and it will be seen that the general result is that there is
no reason at present to believe that Jews are obtaining any
hold on farms.

No doubt the Jew money-lenders, and Pedlars, give credit
to farmers and others, and charge high rates of interest;
but it does not appear that up to the present, at all events,
they have taken mortgages on farms as securities, or in any
way shown a desire to obtain a lien on landed property.

It is quite possible that the explanation of this is
to be found in the fact that the Jews recognise the difficulty in Ireland, in view of the agrarian feeling, of en-
forcing a legal right to land with pecuniary advantage.

If circumstances change, and land once more becomes a

free marketable commodity, Jews would in all probability
accept it as security, and deal in it to their own profit.

With regard to the statement as to Jew tea dealers
dealt with in the Under Secretary's minute of 2nd inst:,
at back, the County Inspectors report without exception,
that there is no reason to believe that Jew tea Pedlars
are in the habit of selling deleterious tea.

Samples of tea sold in County Limerick have been taken
and are at present in the hands of the County Analyst.

Other samples will be taken elsewhere, and a report
furnished later on.

I submit, herewith, a separate report on a return
furnished by the Commissioner of Dublin Metropolitan Police
as to judgments obtained against farmers by Jew money-lenders.

26

N. Chamberlain.

Summary of reports of County Inspectors.

County	No. of Jews in 1891.	No. of Jews in 1901.	Precis of reports
Antrim	2	37	I. A decrease in No. observed since 1901. II. Chiefly travelling pedlars from Belfast. III. They deal mainly with working people - not with farmers. None of them deal in tea.
Armagh	33	44	I. A very slight increase since 1901. II. Mostly Hawkers or Pedlars. III. They deal with poor farmers and work people, and many of these are in debt to them in small sums, paid on the instalment system. No Jew tea dealers.
Belfast	205	708	I. Now about 800 Jews in Belfast. II. Chiefly dealers in furniture, clothes, pictures &c, on the hire instalment system. A few money lenders. III. Some of these travel in the County districts and give credit to small farmers, but not to a large extent. No tea dealers.
Carlow	5	9	I. Now 10 Jews in County. II. Pedlars only. III. They have some of the small farmers in their debt payable by instalments. No tea dealers.
Cavan	2	I	I. No increase. II. Coal and furniture dealer. III. Shopkeeper only. No tea dealer.
Clare	1	0	I. No increase. II. Pedlar. III. Not known to have farmers in debt. No tea sold.
Cork and Cork City	62 155	88 359 }	I. No increase. II. Chiefly Pedlars and small traders on instalment system. III. As Pedlars, have dealings with Country farmers and give them credit. No tea dealers. These figures refer to the whole County of Cork.
Donegal	~	~	I. Three resident in County at present. II. All Pedlars. III. No hold on farmers. No tea dealers.
Down	26	34	I. No increase observed. II. Mainly small Pedlars. III. Several small farmers in their debt on instalment system. No tea dealers.
Dublin County.	86	121	I. Very few resident in County. II. Mainly itinerant Pedlars. III. Farmers incur small debts to them. Some sell tea believed to be genuine.
Fermanagh		3	I. No increase. II. Dealers in old clothes. III. No debts of importance and no tea dealers.
Galway E.R.			I. II. } Nil III.
Galway W.R.		I	I. II. } Nil III.

DOCUMENT 5
COUNTY
INSPECTORS'
REPORTS

Results of investigations into allegations of moneylending and selling 'deleterious' tea

continued on next two pages

County	No. of Jews in 1891.	No. of Jews in 1901.	Precis of reports
Kerry	I3	8	I. Only three Jews in County now. II. All Pedlars. III. Few debts and no tea dealers..
Kildare	*15*	8	I. Increase of one Jew since I901. II. Small dealers and Pedlars, mostly located at Newbridge. III. Deal mainly with the Military. No tea dealers.
Kilkenny	*1*	*2*	I. No increase. II. Pedlars and small dealers. III. Few debts by farmers. No tea dealers.
King's Co.	6	9	I. No increase. II. Mainly Pedlars. III. No debts by farmers and no tea dealers.
Leitrim	2	-	None in County now.
Limerick City and County	93	I7I	I. Slight increase since I901. II. Small shopkeepers in Limerick and Pedlars. III. Deal with farmers on the instalment system. Several tea dealers. Samples of tea sold are being analyzed.
Londonderry *& City*	*5*	*64*	I. Increase of two since I901. II. Small dealers, picture framers &c. One Loan Bank. III. Money lent to farmers on weekly payment system. No tea dealers.
Longford	ـ	*3*	I. Five now in County. II. All Pedlars. III. No serious debts. No tea dealers.
Louth	7	54	I. No. has increased. II. Mainly Pedlars and small dealers. III. Dealers on instalment system with small farmers. No tea dealers.
Mayo	2	-	I. II. } Nil III. }
Meath	*3*	*13*	I. No increase. II. Small trader. One betting man. III. No serious debts. No tea dealers.
Managhan	7	6	I. But two resident Jews in County. II. All Pedlars. III. Small debts only. No tea dealers.
Queen's	9	3	I. No increase. II. All Pedlars. III. No debts. No tea dealers.

County	No. of Jews in 1891.	No. of Jews in 1901.	Precis of reports
Roscommon	I	⊥	I. ⎫ II. ⎬ Nil III. ⎭ .
Sligo	3	14	I. An increase of two. II. Shopkeepers in Sligo town, dealing in furniture, drapery &c. III. Small debts. No tea dealers.
Tyrone	2	2	I. No increase. II. Small shopkeeper and Pedlar. III. No debts . No tea dealer.
Westmeath	I	3	I. No increase. II. Itinerant Pedlars. III. No debts. No tea dealers.
Wexford	I8	I5	I. No increase. II. All small dealers. III. No debts. No tea dealers.
Wicklow	I8	I5	I. No decrease since I901. II. Small shopkeepers and Pedlars. III. No serious debts. Tea dealers in Bray district. Samples will be taken.
Waterford	15	42	I No increase, II. all reside in City of Waterford small dealers. III. No serious debts. no tea dealers

Economic and Social Conditions in Limerick

The 1901 census recorded the population of Limerick city as 38,151 persons, almost 1,000 more than ten years earlier, but only two-thirds of the high of 53,448 in 1851.[60] In common with most major centres outside Dublin, Limerick's population had fallen steadily after the Great Famine.[61] The reasons were similar to those experienced throughout post-famine Ireland: high emigration and late marriages arising from near stagnant general economic conditions. Yet Limerick in the nineteenth century was, according to Willie Gleeson, noted for the 'great number' of what were termed 'home industries', so-called because they manufactured or processed native produce almost in its entirety. An array of industrial concerns, ranging from textiles manufacturing to breweries, from foundries to shipyards, to mills, tanneries, mines, and quarries, provided employment for almost 14,000. But, by the dawn of the twentieth century, many of these 'had ceased to exist'.[62]

Against this background, economic prospects for those of no property in Limerick city and county were quite limited. In the county – the hinterland for the Jewish pedlars – general conditions of the lower classes were poor, and their prospects not great due to a loose labour market influenced by migrant agricultural and domestic labour. William O'Brien reported to the Royal Commission on Labour in 1893 that due to emigration the supply of labourers was insufficient. The farmers suggested that workers who accepted 'reasonable wages need seldom be idle', while labourers claimed farmers only required them for busy months.[63] It was at the hiring fairs of Kilmallock and Newcastle West that local labour met with, and often lost out to, competition from surrounding counties, mainly Kerry. Farmers benefited to the tune of exacting as much as twelve-hour days including board from the servant boys and girls, and the spailpíní fanacha.[64] There were also hiring fairs in the city. The able hoped to obtain the rate of a shilling-a-day with 'legs under the table'; those unable to work hoped to hire out their children.

This 'de-industrialisation' of Limerick had of course been in progress for some time and some of the socio-economic consequences would contribute to events in 1904. In Limerick city, P. J. Ryan noted in his pre-civil war portrait that 'Poverty and near-destitution were commonplace'.[65] Contrary to many reassuring generalisations concerning universal literacy in Ireland, 'total illiteracy was commonplace amongst the poor' in Limerick. Poverty kept many children out of school: some because their parents could not afford it, others because their parents needed child labour to supplement the family income. However, as Ryan noted, 'Whether literate or illiterate public credulity was strong and belief in the clergy was absolute'.[66]

In the circumstances, not surprisingly, the 'financial barometers' of the city were the pawnbrokers who prospered in hard times, gradually recouping their money in improved economic conditions. There were about a dozen pawnshops in the city run by proprietors known as

'Uncles' who, it appears, operated at a profit margin of about twenty per cent each week. The pattern of poverty, as reflected in pawnbroking, was cyclical: Mondays were the highpoint of activity, tapering off until Thursdays when those facing redundancy on Friday pawned their valuables, and those who had money redeemed what they could over the weekend. The patterns of poverty also crossed over into some public houses which gave credit, or 'tick'. Ryan's cross-referencing of debtors in both pawnbrokers and publicans' ledgers revealed that 'there were many families who lived on "tick"'.[67] There were many fathers who deprived their families of the semblance of decency by squandering the meagre income in the public houses of Limerick. The Catholic bishop of Limerick, Edward Thomas O'Dwyer, 'used the pulpit of his own church, and encouraged the Redemptorists to preach to the confraternity, on the abuses of alcohol and other vices that undermined social and moral responsibility and behaviour'.[68] It was precisely in the context of one of those addresses to the arch-confraternity in Limerick that Fr John Creagh stirred up events in January 1904.

Fr John Creagh
and Anti-Semitism

Fr John Creagh took over as director of the arch-confraternity in 1902 at the age of thirty-two; he was the first Limerick-born priest to hold the office.[69] A contemporary article in the *Northern Whig* newspaper described him as an 'athletic, clean-built "figure of a man", with the characteristic cheerfulness and frankness of a son of the soil'.[70] Creagh has been portrayed by the Redemptorist priest, Samuel Boland, as follows:

Fr John
Creagh

*Photograph courtesy
of Limerick Museum*

His preaching was irresistible, said Sister Ignatius, a St John of God who remembered him vividly up to her death. One dour North of Ireland Protestant used to come each Sunday 'to sit under Fr Creagh', ostentatiously leaving the church after the sermon. He spared no one, and the people just loved it, regularly overflowing the church into the street.[71]

This description well fitted the man who was warmly received at his first arch-confraternity meeting in 1902 with the 'customary [Roman] salute'.[72]

From the outset, Creagh's preaching style was demagogic and revivalist, as can be seen by the manner in which he addressed the question of alcohol abuse in the city:

I need not, my dear men, tell you that the great evil of today is drink ... There are publicans who have no conscience – no scruples ... What appeals to their conscience? Money – blood money. Money, the price of souls – the money of Judas. Judas sold his Master for thirty pieces of silver, and these publicans will sell souls, that Jesus Christ died to redeem, for the sake even of a pint of stout or a half glass of whiskey. Appeal to their conscience! Nothing would appeal to their conscience but the prison cell – the lash of the convict.[73]

In early 1904 those same forensic skills were directed against the Jews in the city.[74] It would appear that the priest had been approached by shopkeepers in the city who were hostile to the Jewish pedlars because they provided unwelcome competition. Although the topic of his sermon was not publicised, members of the arch-confraternity had been warned in advance to attend the

JEWISH TRADING

ITS GROWTH IN LIMERICK.

ADDRE-S TO THE CONFRATERNITY

BY FATHER CREAGH, C SS.R.

AT the weekly meeting of the Arch-Confraternity of the Holy Family on Monday evening, and again last evening, some startling statements were made by the Rev. Director concerning the Jewish colony in Limerick and its trade dealings. There was an exceedingly large attendance of members on both evenings; and by arrangement none but members of the Confraternity were admitted to the Church.

Father Creagh, addressing the members of the Arch-Confraternity, said—In beginning to speak to you to-night the first thought that would naturally come to one's mind is what about Christian charity? Does not the law of Our Lord Jesus Christ bind us to love all men, to look upon men as our brothers, and even to do good to those who hate or persecute us. And again has not our own Irish Nation ever been distinguished by its hospitality to the stranger and for its sympathy with the oppressed. Yes; truly Our Lord does bind us to love even our enemies, to do good to all, and our Nation stands pre-eminent by its hospitality and by the *caed mille failthe* that is ever on its lips. But the law of charity never interfered with or lessened a law of nature - the law of self-preservation. Individual self-sacrifice is permitted and even necessary at times. The common good and welfare of a community can never be sacrificed, but must be guarded and defended, and when a common danger is pointed out all are bound to do their utmost to avert it and preserve themselves. It would be madness for a man to nourish in his own breast a viper that might at any moment slay its benefactor with its poisonous bite. So, too, is it madness for a people to allow an evil to grow in their midst that will eventually cause them ruin. Now, to what danger then did he allude to-night—what evil did he wish to direct their attention? It was that they were allowing themselves to become the slaves of Jew usurers. They knew who these were. The Jews were once the chosen people of God. God's mercy and favours towards them were boundless. They were the people of whom was born the Messiah, Jesus Christ. Our Lord and Master. But they rejected Jesus — they crucified Him—they called down the curse of His precious blood upon their own heads—''His blood be upon us and our children'' they cried and that curse came upon them. They were scattered over the earth after the siege of Jerusalem, A D 70; and they bore away with them an unquenchable hatred of the name of Jesus Christ and His followers. They persecuted the Christians from the beginning. They slew St Stephen, the First Martyr, and St James the Apostle, and ever since as often as opportunity offered they did not hesitate to shed Christian blood, and that even in the meanest and most cruel manner as in the case of the holy martyr St Simeone, who though a mere child they took and crucified out of hatred and derision towards Our Lord Jesus Christ. Nowadays they dare not kidnap and slay Christian children, but they will not hesitate to expose them to a longer and even more cruel martyrdom by taking the clothes off their back and the bit out of their mouths. Twenty years ago and less Jews were known only by name and evil repute in Limerick. They were sucking the blood of other nations, but those nations rose up and turned them out. And they came to our land to fasten themselves on us like leeches and to draw our blood when they had been forced away from other countries. They have, indeed, fastened themselves upon us; and now the question is whether or not we will allow them to fasten themselves still more upon us, until we and our children are the helpless victims of rapacity. The Jews came to Limerick apparently the most miserable tribe imaginable, with want on their faces, but now they had enriched themselves and could boast of very considerable house property in the city. Their rags have been exchanged for silk. They have wormed themselves into every form of business. They are in the furniture trade, the mineral water trade, the milk trade, the drapery trade, and in fact into business of every description, and traded even under Irish names. Just a few minutes ago I was handed a copy of the '' Chronicle'' with an account of a Jewish wedding. Listen to what it says—'' At the Synagogue, inside and out, were large crowds, the difference between them being that whereas those outside (most of them) wore poverty's motley, those inside were clad in fine broadcloth in silks and satins goodly to look upon. From the outside to the door of the Synagogue itself choice decorations were displayed, and the feet of the maiden trod as dainty a carpet as ever was laid down in the most 'fashionable' edifice in the country.'' Mark the words—''those outside (most of them) wore poverty's motley.'' This certainly tells its own tale How do the Jews manage to make money? Some of you may know their methods better than I do, but still it is my duty to expose their methods. They go about as pedlars from door to door, pretending to offer articles at very cheap prices, but in reality charging several times the value more than they were bought in the shops. The Jew is most persevering and barefaced in his statement as to the value of his goods. He does not mind to whom he offers his wares. A few weeks ago I was standing with three other priests at the door of a priest's house, when a Jew had the boldness to walk up to us, and had the great kindness to offer to furnish us with the latest modern songs. That will show you how they push their trade. They force themselves and their goods upon the people, and the people are blind as to their tricks. Then they had the weekly payment system. They offer an article several times its value, and they are content to have it paid off by small instalments every week. The result is the article is paid for again and again, and people when they are caught and trapped grow tired of paying such unjust demands, refuse to pay, and most commonly are unable to pay, and then comes the inevitable summons and the bailiffs. When the summons is for less than £1 16s 8d it must go before the Mayor's Court of Conscience; if for a larger sum it goes before another court. Then a decree is given, and the Mayor's sergeants are forced to become collectors of money for the Jews, and the bailiffs are put in, and the little property seized and sold by the rapacious Jews The victims of the Jews are mostly the women of a house. The Jew has got a sweet tongue when he wishes—he passes off his miserable goods upon her. She has to spare and stint to get the

DOCUMENT 6
MUNSTER
NEWS, 13
JANUARY 1904

Report on Fr Creagh's sermon in which he attacked the Jews for their alleged exploitation of Limerick's poor

continued on next page

35

money to pay off the Jew without her husband knowing it, and then follow misery, sorrow and deceit. The wife is afraid lest her husband should find out that she had been dealing with the Jews. The Jew makes his appearance while the husband is in the house. The shilling is slipped into his hand—he goes away, the shilling is not marked down—no credit is given for it and this unregistered payment is made again a law suit. The wife, too, will beg the Jew not to come to her house—she does not want him to be seen coming, and then stealthy visits must be paid at night, in the darkness, lest the dealings might be found out. Stand at a prominent Jew's house at night, and you will be surprised to see the number and the class of people who are going in and out, under cover of shawls, to pay the Jew his usury. Servant girls, too, are the common dupes of the designing Jew—cheap, gaudy jewellery, showy dresses, are passed off on her, and thus her scanty earnings are swallowed up by the Hebrew. Nor does the Jew care what exposure he makes to carry on his business—he is contented to carry on his business in the dark, if necessary, but after that comes the court day. Visit the Mayor's Court on a Thursday—you may not see it now for some time, for the Jews may hold their hands —but if you visited it during the past two years you would think it was a special court for the whole benefit of the Jews. I have here in my possession an authentic document containing a list of the summonses issued by the Jews during the past two years. I will read the number of summonses, with the amounts sued for, week after week. (Here Father Creagh read the paper giving the weekly returns of the Court). In 1902 some 337 summonses were issued for £303 1s 1d in 1903, 226 summonses for £172 11s 4d. Surely this reveals a terrible state of things. It so many people had to be sued for money week after week, and for sums under £1 16s 8d, how many people must, we conclude, are constantly dealing with them. And these figures do not deal with proces ses in the other courts. The Jews do not confine themselves to the city. They have made Limerick their headquarters from which they can spread their rapacious nets over the country all round. When they came here first they had to carry their packs upon their shoulders. Now they can afford to have horses and traps to carry their goods, and they can go long distances by train, and succeed in making the farmers their dupes as well as those living in the towns To make their traffic easier they will barter in kind instead of in money. They will take a hen, or a goose, or a turkey, eggs or butter, and people will thus only receive half the market value of their poultry and dairy produce. Again if the Jews bought their goods in the city they might be of some benefit. But do they deal with local traders? They do to a certain extent, but they prefer to get their goods from other Jews across the Channel, and week by week tons of goods of every description are landed in Limerick from Jews outside the country, and thus the Jews cripple local trade and industry. For instance the furniture made in London deprives the local tradesmen of their work and the weekly wage to support their family. The Jews lend money in time of need, but at what rate of interest. Let me enter into a few figures. If you want £5 you get not the £5, but £4 1s 3d, or 18s 9d less, which means 75 per cent at the end of the year. In the Pery Jubilee offices you are only charged 4d in the pound. In the banks the charge is five per cent. so you only pay £4 5s at the end of the year, whereas you have to pay something like double the amount borrowed from the Jews Is not this robbery, and are we to be made fools of in this country for ever? Are the Jews a help to religion. I do not hesitate to say that there are no greater enemies of the Catholic Church than the Jews. Yet you will see the Jew carrying through town and country pictures of our Divine Lord, crucifixes, statues, and pictures of the Blessed Virgin Mary. This very day a man told me that not long ago he saw a Jew selling pictures of Our Lord, and as he walked along, when he thought no one heard him, he was blasphem-

ing the Holy Name of Jesus. If you want an example look to France. What is going on at present in that land? The little children are being deprived of their education. No Nun, Monk, or Priest can teach in a school. The little ones are forced to go where God's name is never mentioned—to go to Godless schools. The Jews are in league with the Freemasons in France, and have succeeded in burning out of that country all the nuns and religious orders. The Redemptorist Fathers to the number of two hundred had been turned out of France, and that is what the Jews would do in our own country if they are allowed to get into power. To say nothing of charges of immorality brought against the Jews by distributing to innocent country people indecent pictures impure books, and aiding corruption of morals in other ways, for these things are hard to be proved, for the guilty one must carry on his unlawful practice in a manner that cannot be detected lest he might be punished by the law. In conclusion, he advised advised them to have no dealings in the manner he had described, with the Jews. If they had any transactions with them they should get out of them as soon as possible, and then afterwards keep far away from them.

Monday meeting (mass) on 11 January in large numbers. Creagh began innocently enough by talking about Christian charity and the duty to look upon all men as brothers, even those who hate or persecute Christians:

> [but] it would be madness for a man to nourish in his own breast a viper that might at any moment slay a benefactor with its poisonous bite. So too is it madness for a people to allow an evil to grow in their midst that will eventually cause them ruin.[75]

He then launched into what became the theme of the evening, and was widely reported in the press as reflected by the coverage given in the *Munster News* (document 6).

His theme was an attack on the Jews, retrospective and contemporary, rounding on alleged exploitation of the poor of Limerick. During his sermon, Creagh dramatically produced a copy of the *Limerick Chronicle* which had just been handed to him. He read to his congregation the account of a recent Jewish wedding – in fact the wedding of Fanny Toohey and Maurice B. Massell the previous Thursday. This wedding may have indirectly contributed to the growing tension between local residents and a section of the Jewish community. Fanny Goldberg, who was eleven at the time, remembered it well; she recorded in her unpublished memoirs how childish curiosity took her uninvited (the schism in the Jewish community meant that the Goldbergs had not been on the guest list) to the synagogue to see the bride:

> It was the usual kind of wedding with the horse drawn carriages and white satin clad bride, and satin clad brides- maids. And all men in top and of course the guests in their

best. I thought the bridesmaids were beautiful in their long dresses, and coloured satin capes trimmed with swans down. There was a crowd of onlookers outside the [synagogue], with women in ragged shawls, and overawed barefoot children. It was said at the time that this display of 'silks and satins' put the light to the smouldering fire.

That may or may not have been the case. But Creagh made the most of it. Reading from the *Limerick Chronicle* report, he recounted how outside the synagogue were those who wore 'poverty's motley', while those inside 'were clad in fine broadcloth, and silks and satins goodly to look upon'. Creagh asked how Jews managed to make this money, implying unscrupulous and immoral methods. He also highlighted the evil of the weekly payments system where the client was often unable to make the repayments and alleged that housewives were mostly the victims. He invited members of the congregation to stand at a prominent Jew's house at night and observe those coming and going covertly. Creagh told the congregation that he had an authentic document containing a list of the summonses issued by Jews during the past two years, which he duly read and contrasted the cost of credit from Jews with lending institutions. Even the countryside was not safe, he warned, as the Jew pedlars sold their imported wares there.

He advised his congregation to have no commercial dealings with Jews, terminate ongoing transactions and strictly avoid them.[76] In the country that invented the phrase, this was nothing short of a call for a boycott.

The Impact of Fr Creagh's Sermon: Boycott of Limerick Jews

Colooney Street (subsequently Wolfe Tone Street), where most Limerick Jews lived, was only a few minutes walk from the Redemptorist church. The hundreds who left the church after the meeting had to pass the top of Colooney Street on their way home; many were fired up by Creagh's incendiary sermon. The Jewish community immediately sensed the menacing mood of the crowd turned mob and remained locked in their homes as the church militants passed by. Jewish shops,

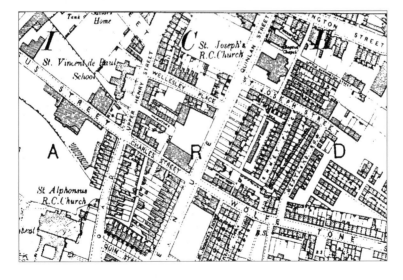

MAP OF JEWISH QUARTER IN LIMERICK CITY

St Alphonsus Church was the Redemptorist church at which Fr Creagh gave his sermon; leaving the church and walking east would have brought the congregation right through the Jewish quarter of Limerick.

however, remained open and their owners felt menaced. One old Fenian – a member of the confraternity – single-handedly defended a shop from attack until the police arrived to mount a guard.

FROM THE——

merick Hebrew Congregation,

SYNAGOGUE CHAMBERS,

COLOONEY STREET.

Limerick, January 13th 1904

No. 122

To County Inspector Hayes R.I.C.
Limerick

DOCUMENT 7
13 JANUARY
1904

*Rabbi Levin's
letter to the RIC
drawing their
attention to the
unrest caused by
Fr Creagh's
speech*

Dear Sir

As Officiating Minister of the Limerick Hebrew Congregation it is my duty to draw your attention to the following

In consequence of an address delivered by Father Creagh, a copy of which I herewith enclose I beg to inform you That every member of my Community regards his life at this moment in peril. as a matter of fact several of us have been already in this two foregone days insulted assaulted, and abused with menacing language Therefore I beg of you dear Sir on behalf of my Community to secure them ample protection viz., To have constables posted in every street in all parts of the City. Though bycoted by the Priest lecture they are obliged to go about everywhere in order to earn a living

Thanking you in anticipation

I remain respectfully Yours

E B Levin

18 Coloney Str.

DOCUMENT 8
HAYES' ORDER
AND O'HARA'S
REPORT

*Hayes instructed
O'Hara to make
arrangements
with the local
police to prevent
the Jews 'being
molested'*

14.1. 1904

With reference to the attached Speech made by Father Creagh. You will make such arrangement with the local police as to prevent their being Molested. Let me Know your arrangement

Mr Hayes

continued on next page

The D.I. Limerick

Limerick 18.1.04

I beg to
report that I have directed
special attention to be paid
to the Jews by all the city
stations especially next monday
when they collect instalments
(weekly) due to them. I went
to Boherbuoy & Docks stations
yesterday & gave the Sergeants
special instructions as to
looking after the Jews &
affording them every protection.

I also visited Mr. Levin,
one of the Rabbis, in Colooney St.
& asked him to let his
people know that they
would get every assistance
from the police & also to
report to us any
cases of assault or abuse
of Jews that took place.

It would be well to
send out word to stations
in the county that the Jews
usually leave Limerick on
monday to collect their
instalments through the county.

DOCUMENT 8
continued

The report noted
the measures
O'Hara had
taken to prevent
violence against
the Jewish
population

Fearing an all-out attack on his community, Rabbi Ellas Bere Levin wrote to Irish political leaders and to Jewish organisations in England asking for their public support. He told Michael Davitt in a letter on 15 January that the priest's allegations were 'devoid of any particle of truth' and set out a clearer record. Levin asked Davitt to conclude for himself whether the anti-Semitic outburst had its roots in religious prejudices or had been 'promoted by local traders', and sought his intervention to avert a general boycott and rioting.

Rabbi Levin also sought police protection for the Jewish community from further intimidation. On 13 January, he sent a report of Creagh's sermon and an earnest plea on behalf of his community to the Royal Irish Constabulary (RIC) county inspector, Thomas Hayes (document 7).

In response, District Inspector C. H. O'Hara was instructed on 14 January to make 'such arrangements with the local police as to prevent their [the Jews] being molested'. O'Hara reported on 16 January of the measures he had implemented including a visit to Rabbi Levin at his home in Colooney Street (document 8).

On 18 January Michael Davitt's immediate response to Rabbi Levin's letter of 15 January was published in the *Freeman's Journal*. Davitt robustly refuted Creagh's claims in an open letter that included Rabbi Levin's original correspondence (see document 9). Creagh would later – in his second sermon – return to Davitt's rebuttal of allegations regarding ritual killing. Praising the bishop of Limerick, Dr Edward Thomas O'Dwyer, Davitt encouraged Rabbi Levin to seek a meeting with him.[77]

THE JEWS IN LIMERICK.

LETTER FROM MR. DAVITT.

TO THE EDITOR OF THE FREEMAN.

Sir—I will ask you to allow me a little of your space to deal with a matter which is in my humble judgment one of public concern to all who love and revere the Catholic religion, and who have no less a degree of affection for the name and honour of Ireland.

It has been the unique glory of our country that its original conquest to the cause of Christianity was effected without bloodshed, while the sons of St. Patrick have truly upheld that reputation from then till now. Irish Catholics have suffered every possible form of religious oppression known to the perverted ingenuity of the authors of the Penal Code; but it is their proud boast that neither in Ireland nor in any land to which English rule has forced them to fly did they ever resort to a counter-religious persecution.

In the year 1747, or thereabouts, the Irish House of Commons, in rebuke to a then anti-Jewish outbreak in England, openly condemned such un-Christian violence, and extended a welcome to oppressed Jews to the shelter of the then laws of Ireland.

A few years ago, perhaps a dozen, the Chief Rabbi of London, on a visit to Dublin, declared that when he set foot on Irish soil he was in the only land in Europe in which his race had never suffered persecution.

The accompanying letter explains these observations.

In the sermon or speech referred to, which has been fully reported in the Limerick papers, I find the following words:—

"They slew St. Stephen the First Martyr and St. James the Apostle, and ever since as often as opportunity offered they did not hesitate to shed Christian blood, and that even in the meanest and most cruel manner, as in the case of the holy martyr, St. Simeone, who though a mere child, they took and crucified out of hatred and derision towards Our Lord Jesus Christ. Nowadays they dare not kidnap and slay Christian children, but they will not hesitate to expose them to a longer and even more cruel martyrdom by taking the clothes off their back and the bit out of their mouths. Twenty years ago and less Jews were known only by name and evil repute in Limerick. They were sucking the blood of other nations, but these nations rose up and turned them out, and they came to our land to fasten themselves on us like leeches and to draw our blood when they had been forced away from other countries. They have, indeed, fastened themselves upon us, and now the question is whether or not we will allow them to fasten themselves still more upon us, until we and our children are the helpless victims of their rapacity."

"Nowadays they dare not kidnap and slay Christian children." Sir, it was atrocious language like this which, in May last, was responsible for some of the most hideous crimes possible to perverted humanity, in a Russian city.

There is not one atom of truth in the horrible allegation about ritual murder, here insinuated, against this persecuted race. Again and again, to their eternal credit, the Popes of the Middle Ages condemned this invention of sordid purpose or of blind hate, as untrue, un-Christian, and reprehensible, and no Pontiff has ever sanctioned the circulation of these abominable stories, the dissemination of which has led to the slaughter of tens of thousands of innocent lives throughout Europe in past times.

I protest as an Irishman and as a Catholic against this spirit of barbarous malignity being introduced into Ireland, under the pretended form of a material regard for the welfare of our workers. The reverend gentleman complained of the rags and poverty of the children of Limerick, as compared with the prosperity of the Jews, and on this ground deliberately incited the people of that city to hunt the Jews from their midst.

Let me suggest a field for his reforming energies which will not require the invocation of any poisonous feeling of racial animosity or of un-Christian hate. Let him attack the English rule of Ireland which levies £12,000,000 of taxes every year, on our lives and industries, not to the good, but to the injury, of our country. Let him try and induce the people of this country to save a few millions every year out of the ten millions spent needlessly on intoxicating drink. Let him do work of this kind for the good of Limerick and the progress of Ireland, and the rags he complains of and the poverty he deplores will, if he is successful, vanish far more effectively, and sooner, than by preaching a cowardly vendetta of anti-Semitic prejudice.

Fortunately Limerick is a stronghold of true Nationalist sentiment, and cannot be induced to dishonour Ireland by any response to such unworthy and un-Catholic invitations.

Limerick also has a Bishop of splendid intellectual powers, who is a great Churchman, whatever faults some of us occasionally find with him in relation to other questions, and it is certain that a mind as clear, and a reputation such as his, will not allow the fair name of Catholic Ireland to be sullied through an anti-Jewish crusade, under his spiritual jurisdiction, to the injury and shame of a city of which every Irishman is historically proud.—I remain, yours truly,

MICHAEL DAVITT.

Dalkey, January 16, 1904.

DOCUMENT 9
FREEMAN'S
JOURNAL
18 JANUARY
1904

Michael Davitt's response to Rabbi Levin's plea on behalf of the Jewish community

The leader of the Irish Parliamentary Party, John Redmond, also replied promptly in defence of the Limerick Jews: 'I have no sympathy whatever with the attacks upon the Hebrew Community in Limerick or elsewhere. I feel sure that the good sense and spirit of toleration of the Irish people will be sufficient to protect them from any wrong.'[78] Levin must have been comforted by the fact that no major figure, no national politician or bishop, rushed to endorse Creagh's anti-Semitic attack.

On 18 January, also, County Inspector Hayes called to see Rabbi Levin, and in his absence requested the rabbi write a report on the current position of the Jews (document 10). Levin thanked the constabulary for their assistance in calming down the situation but also outlined the depressed trading conditions of the community.

On the same day District Inspector O'Hara confirmed that policing was difficult and that the squeeze was on the Jewish traders. However, consultations with the administrator of St Michael's parish, Fr J. Cregan, his curate, Fr John Lee, and the priests of the neighbouring St John's parish, led O'Hara to take an optimistic view of the prospects of an early resolution (document 11).

The spiritual director of the women's confraternity in St John's Cathedral, Fr Murphy, denounced the violence against the Jews but otherwise offered little comfort:

> If the people owed money to the Jews they should pay it as they were bound to pay all their lawful debts. If it was their desire to get rid of the Israelites, this was the best way to accomplish it, and when this was done they need have no more dealings with them.[79]

18 Colooney Str.
Limerick
Jan. 18th 1904

Dear Sir
          I regret I had not the
pleasure of seeing you personally
as you had been so kind to call
upon me this evening,
In comply with your request I will
give you a brief & general
sketch of our present situation. Those of us who trade
on the weekly pament system
are literally ruined, I am
informed that they hardly
collect 10% of their usual
collection; and as for selling
goods that is out of the
question, not one shillings
worth of goods having been
sold by them for the last

– 2 –

fortnight in the City of Limk,
So far as baying goods is co-
cernct, there is no doubt that
a general, baycott prevails,
The people who have hitherto
dealt with the members of
my community say that they
were ordered by Fr. Creagh
neither to pay their debts
nor to purchase goods,
There are six Jewish petty
hucksters shops, whose

*The report
outlined the
present situation
saying that 'those
of us who trade
on the weekly
pament [sic]
system are
literally ruined'*

*continued on
next two pages*

...shops, whose owners until now managed to live, but whose ruin is already visible, having lost all their Christian custom since the first address on Jewish Trade was delivered.

-3-

by Fr. Creagh, Whilst on the other hand, they are greatly pressed with bills by those wholesale shop keepers with whom they have dealt for years on credit, and who had always placed the greatest confidence in them, To give you an idea — though the remotest — of their situation I will mention one fact Two of these petty shop-keepers do a little in the milk trade, one of whom dealt for years with a Mr. Gleeson of Kilpeacon Road. The latter used to supply him ten or twelve gallons of milk daily

4

and since last fortnig. he refused to do so any more, The other petty shop keeper. who also deals a little in the milk tread has been given notice by the farmer who ... hitherto to supply him *with milk that he will not supply him any more. So much for the Jewish business in Limerick.*

With regard to violence I must say, that thanks to the police protection afforded us, there is hardly any incident worth complaining of, excepting insults and abusive language given us to which we are no aliens, —

I remain yours respectfully

E.B.Levin

Thomas Hayes Esq.
County Inspector
R.I.C.

An editorial in the *Limerick Leader*, which appeared on the evening of 18 January, was supportive of the boycott but sought to calm matters in the city in the interest of fair play (document 12).

That same evening Rabbi Levin's outlook altered dramatically between writing to County Inspector Hayes in the morning and cabling the chief rabbi in London, Dr Ernest W. Harris: 'Anti-Semitic riots took place through the day. General boycott in force. Community in peril. Every member assaulted.[80] A special correspondent for the *Jewish Chronicle*, reporting from the city on 18 January, wrote fearfully about what was likely to happen, and thought he was back again in the Middle Ages, hearing:

> the miserable cry: 'Down with the Jews!' 'Death to the Jews!' 'We must hunt them out' is still ringing in my ears,

and sends a cold shiver through my body. Today, Monday, the chief business day, Jews were attacked right and left. I myself witnessed one scene where a Jew was actually running for his life, and as he passed through one crowd he was actually hemmed in by another, till the police came on the scene. But that is only one case out of many! And this in a land of freedom, this in the twentieth century, this only two weeks after Christmas, when peace and goodwill to all mankind was preached throughout the land!

The correspondent concluded on a depressing note:

When I witnessed the organised attacks today and heard the mob yell 'Down with the Jews: they kill our innocent children', all the horrors of Kishineff came back to me, and then, and only then, was I able to realise what Kishineff meant [referring to the 1903 pogrom in Kishbinev, Bessarabia in Russia].[81]

The *Jewish Chronicle* wrote that 'the Jews of Limerick are living in a state of terror' and that Rabbi Levin feared 'a general boycott, and perhaps a regular anti-Semitic riot'.[82] The 'regular anti-Semitic riot' was not to happen.

DISTRICT INSPECTOR'S OFFICE,

LIMERICK. 18·1·03

Submitted a
cutting from "Freeman's Journal"
of this date containing a
letter from Mr. Levin, Rabbi
of the Jewish community here,
to Mr. Davitt & a letter from
the latter to the "Freeman" in
reply. I reported on 16th inst.
the steps I had taken to
look after the Jews. To-day
a number of them - about 40 -
went about collecting their
instalments & in most cases
got nothing but abuse. Crowds
followed them hooting &, in
some cases, throwing mud at
them. It was difficult to
keep an eye to them all as
they went in many cases
to back streets without the
knowledge of the police. The
names of several persons who
followed them in a disorderly
manner were taken & one boy,
who had picked up a stone
& threw at them, was arrested

DOCUMENT 11
18 JANUARY 1904
O'HARA'S
REPORT

O'Hara reported
that 'a number [of
Jews] went about
collecting their
instalments and in
most cases got
nothing but abuse'
(The date of the
report has been
mis-transcribed by
O'Hara as 18
January 1903
instead of 1904.)

continued on
next page

∂ was, later on, discharged to be summoned to Petty Sessions.

I went this afternoon to Fr. Cregan & Fr. Lee who are in charge of the two largest parishes here. Both these gentlemen exercise a very large influence here & they disapprove of Fr. Creagh's attack entirely & I gathered from them that the latter — who is not one of the parochial clergy but belongs to the Redemptorist order, which has a church here — was not authorized by any one to speak as he did.

Fr. Cregan & Fr. Lee will advise their people not to interfere with or molest the Jews & I think after a while that the excitement will subside.

Special measures have been taken to protect the houses in the Jewish quarter.

I also enclose a cutting from "Limerick Leader" of this evening which advises people to avoid violence &c. towards the Jews.

C. Hotham, 21

LIMERICK LEADER.

MONDAY EVENING, JANUARY 18, 1904.

HEAR ALL SIDES.

In another column of our issue this evening we insert Mr. DAVITT's letter to the *Freeman's Journal* on the subject of the Rev. Father CREAGH's recent remarks on the Jewish community in Limerick. In giving the letter publicity we are not to be taken as adopting his views, our desire being merely to show all sides fair play. In fact we are fully inclined to leave to Father CREAGH himself the framing of a reply to the writer of the epistle, believing as we do that the rev gentleman is better in a position to do so than ourselves. One thing, however, we regret, and it is this, that Mr. DAVITT did not treat on Father CREAGH's remarks more generally instead of confining himself to a small extract which has the tendency of obscuring the issue at stake, or, at all events, making less clear the objects which prompted them. Having said so much, we again desire to point out that the hospitality of our columns is open to both sides. Our motive is fair play and nothing more. The policy of the LIMERICK LEADER is now too well known to create the feeling that we are actuated by any other interests than those of the common weal. One word more. It has come to our knowledge that the Jews for the past few days have been subjected to ill-treatment and assault while passing through our public thoroughfares. We regret that such has been the case. We are living in critical times when every advantage is taken by unscrupulous opponents to misinterpret our acts and the cause of our religion. In such a crisis it is not wise to give a handle to vilification. If the people do not want the Jews, then leave them severely alone. Above all things have no recourse to violence. Such a policy only shows weakness, if not foolish vindictiveness, and will never succeed in accomplishing that which is, or may be desired.

DOCUMENT 12
18 JANUARY 1904
EDITORIAL IN
LIMERICK LEADER

The editorial urged people not to 'give a handle to vilification', but saying that 'If people do not want the Jews, then leave them severely alone'

Fr Creagh's Second Anti-Semitic Sermon: 18 January 1904

Fr Creagh's sermon on Monday 18 January attracted international press attention.[83] Though members of the arch-confraternity were instructed to prevent journalists from being present at their meeting, the text of his sermon was published in the local papers the following day.[84] Creagh entered the pulpit to loud applause from the congregation. While seeking to be conciliatory in view of the disturbances in the city during the day, his sermon confirmed that he was an intransigent and unrepentant anti-Semite. Creagh condemned the violence towards Jews but used injudicious language that only went to heighten and inflame emotions against Jews. He then read out Davitt's letter in defence of the Jewish community and denied he had ever insinuated ritual

DOCUMENT 13
19 JANUARY 1904
ARTICLE IN
LIMERICK ECHO

The article
included Michael
Davitt's letter in
support of the Jews
and Fr Creagh's
second anti-
Semitic speech
responding to
Davitt

continued on
next two pages

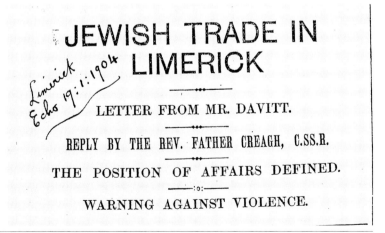

JEWISH TRADE IN LIMERICK

Limerick Echo 19:1:1904

LETTER FROM MR. DAVITT.

REPLY BY THE REV. FATHER CREAGH, C.SS.R.

THE POSITION OF AFFAIRS DEFINED.

WARNING AGAINST VIOLENCE.

At the weekly meeting of the Arch-Confraternity of the Holy Family at the Redemptorist Church last night, the Rev. Father Creagh, C.SS.R., Spiritual Director, referred at length to the letter from Mr Michael Davitt, which appeared in yesterday's *Freeman* on the subject of Jewish trade in Limerick, to which attention was drawn by Father Creagh at the Confraternity last week. At the beginning of his remarks last night,

Father Creagh said he desired it to be thoroughly understood that he entirely and fully deprecated any violence towards the Jews. Such was never his intention, and he felt sure his advice on the matter would be followed by the people. Violence of any kind would only ruin the people's cause. The only reason for which he took up this question was merely to save the Confraternity men from the ruinous trade of the Jews and the Jewish religion, as a religion had nothing whatever to do with his statements. He noticed that the *Munster News* had stated that last week "the church by arrangement was kept with closed doors." That was not so, but every member knew that the church on Monday and Tuesday nights was only open for members of the Confraternity or those who intended to join it, and no one but members had a right to come in their. Only this rule was enforced on Monday and Tuesday night last.

MR. DAVITT'S LETTER.

Continuing, the Rev. Father Creagh said—

At the last meeting I warned you to beware of becoming the slaves of Jewish usurers. I pointed out to you that the Jews were ever the greatest haters of the name of Jesus Christ, and of everything Christian. I told you how they had wormed themselves into every form of business—that, whereas they had come here a miserable tribe, they had enriched themselves upon our poverty, and I asked you to consider well whether or not we were to allow them to fasten themselves so tightly on us that we and our children should be the helpless victims of their rapacity. My address to you was reported in the public Press, and has caused no small sensation in the country at large, for, as the *Daily Independent* says,

> "It is a question of more than local interest, and one that will require to be dealt with sooner or later. There are few things more remarkable in the recent history of Ireland than the extraordinary extent to which the Jews have invaded the country. At the present moment they seem to swarm all over the land, and their peculiar methods of business have become very unpleasantly felt in the various centres of population. They have settled down in large numbers in Dublin, Belfast, and apparently also in other Irish cities and towns, and the undesirable state of things described by Father Creagh is certainly very typical by all accounts of the state of affairs prevailing in many other localities."

If Limerick is typical of other localities as regards Jewish methods, all then I can say is God help our nation and our race, unless something is done, and done speedily also, to change such a deplorable state of things. Now being responsible, as I am, for the welfare of so many thousands of men and boys, and seeing the greatness of the evil that stares us in the face, I would consider myself a traitor to my religion or my country if I did not raise my voice, even though I stood alone, against such an evil. I knew very well that

I WOULD BE THE OBJECT OF MUCH BITTER ATTACK

from the enemies of God and from those who had been duped by the Jews, by those who were in their bands and wanted to screen themselves; but I did not expect such a letter from Mr Davitt as appeared in this day's issue of the *Freeman*. I will say nothing about Mr Davitt, or as to his motives in writing such a letter. I will give him credit for the highest, but as his letter may be against the common good,

I AM SURELY BOUND TO MAKE SOME REPLY.

I will read his letter for you. Mr Davitt writes:—

"TO THE EDITOR OF THE FREEMAN.

"SIR—I will ask you to allow me a little of your space to deal with a matter which is in my humble judgment one of public concern to all who love and revere the Catholic religion, and who have no less a degree of affection for the name and honour of Ireland."

I thoroughly agree with Mr Davitt that this is a matter, in my humble judgment, "one of public concern to all who love and revere the Catholic religion, and who have no less a degree of affection for the name and honour of Ireland." That is, just as I stated, why I spoke against the Jewish usurer. Mr Davitt continues:—

"It has been the unique glory of our country that its original conquest to the cause of Christianity was effected without bloodshed, while the sons of St Patrick have truly upheld that reputation from then till now. Irish Catholics have suffered every possible form of religious oppression known to the perverted ingenuity of the authors of the Penal Code, but it is their proud boast that neither in Ireland nor in any land to which English rule has forced them to fly did they ever resort to a counter religious persecution."

Yes, unfortunately Ireland has "suffered every possible form of religious oppression known to the perverted ingenuity of the authors of the Penal Code." But tell me is that the reason why we should voluntarily submit to another and equally cruel

PERSECUTION AT THE HANDS OF THE JEWS,

as Catholics are being persecuted this very day by the power of the Jews and Freemasons of France, where, as I have told you, that all religious orders have been turned out, where their property has been confiscated and seized by the State, and Catholic children forced to go to godless schools, where the name of God, the name of their Creator and Redeemer, Jesus Christ, cannot be mentioned. Nor is the persecution in France anything new.

THE JEWS HAVE ALWAYS BEEN A DANGER TO CHRISTIAN PEOPLE.

They were the cause of the Spanish Inquisition being instituted. I do not want to defend the Spanish Inquisition, but hear what Pastor, a writer of undoubted impartiality, says in History of the Popes:—"This tribunal (the Spanish Inquisition) was created in the first instance to deal with the special circumstances of the Jewish Community in Spain. No other European state had suffered to the extent that Spain was then suffering from the unrelenting system of usury and organised extortion practised by these dangerous aliens. Persecutions were the natural consequence, and often the only ultimatum before the Jews was baptism or death. Thus the number of merely nominal converts to the Christian faith soon became very great. The secret Jews were incomparably more dangerous than those who openly professed their religion. 'If the latter monopolised the greater part of the wealth and commerce of the country, the former threatened alike the Spanish Nationality and the Christian Faith. On the one hand they contrived to insinuate themselves into a number of ecclesiastic charges and even to become Bishops, and on the other to attain high municipal honours, and to marry into all the noble families. These advantages and their great wealth were all covertly devoted to the subjugation of the Spaniards and the undermining of their Faith in favour of the Jews and Judaism. Things had come to such a pass that the interests of Christian Spain was at stake.' The inquisition was created as a remedy for these evils." Pastor quotes Hefele (Xinenes) A Huber, Vol. V. Again surely the Irish people at home and abroad never resorted to a "counter religious persecution," nor can it be said that I asked you to persecute the Jews. All I asked you was to open your eyes, and to see how you were allowing yourselves to be plundered, and to put a stop to the same by

SIMPLY LEAVING THE JEWS SEVERELY ALONE.

Mr Davitt continues:—

"In the year 1747 or thereabouts the Irish House of Commons, in rebuke to the then anti-Jewish outbreak in England, openly condemned such un-Christian violence, and extended a welcome to oppressed Jews to the shelter of the then laws of Ireland."

Does Mr Davitt wish to hold up the Irish Parliament of the eighteenth century as a model Irish Parliament? If so, let him study Mr Lecky's "History of the Eighteenth Century," and he will see that Ireland at that time had no bitterer enemy than its own Parliament.

"A few years ago, perhaps a dozen, the Chief Rabbi of London, on a visit to Dublin, declared that when he set foot on Irish soil he was in the only land in Europe in which his race had never suffered persecution."

Why did the Chief Rabbi say that Ireland was the only country in which his race had never suffered persecution? In the first place remember that we are not persecuting them. But at that time we had not felt the result of the Jewish usurer's trade. It takes some time to have their persecutions thoroughly felt. But why did every other land persecute them? Simply because of the vile practices of the Jews. Again every effect has a cause, and a universal effect must have a universal cause. People do not persecute their friends, but their enemies. Hence is it not only fair to conclude that the Jews have proved themselves to be the enemies of every country in Europe, and every nation had to defend itself against them. Let us defend ourselves before their heels are too firmly planted upon our necks. Again, Mr Davitt writes:—

"In the sermon or speech referred to, which has been fully reported in the Limerick papers, I find the following words:—

"They slew St Stephen the First Martyr and St James the Apostle, and ever since as often as opportunity offered they did not hesitate to shed Christian blood, and that even in the meanest and most cruel manner, as in the case of the holy martyr, St Simeone, who, though a mere child, they took and crucified out of hatred and derision towards Our Lord Jesus Christ. Nowadays they dare not kidnap and slay Christian children, but they will not hesitate to expose them to a longer and even more cruel martyrdom by taking the clothes off their back and the bit out of their mouths. Twenty years ago and less Jews were known only by name and evil repute in Limerick. They were sucking the blood of other nations but these nations rose up and turned them out. And they came to our land to fasten themselves on us like leeches and to draw our blood when they had been forced away from other countries. They have, indeed, fastened themselves upon us, and now the question is whether or not we will allow them to fasten themselves still more upon us, until we and our children are the helpless victims of their rapacity."

"Nowadays they dare not kidnap and slay Christian children." Sir, it was atrocious language like this which, in May last, was responsible for some of the most hideous crimes possible to perverted humanity, in a Russian city.

"There is not one atom of truth in the horrible allegation about ritual murder, here insinuated, against this persecuted race. Again and again, to their eternal credit, the Popes of the Middle Ages condemned this invention of sordid purpose or of blind hate, as untrue, un-Christian, and reprehensible, and no Pontiff has ever sanctioned the circulation of these abominable stories, the dissemination of which has led to the slaughter of tens of thousands of innocent lives throughout Europe in past times."

NOW, I DID NOT INSINUATE RITUAL MURDER.

I protest against such a false assertion, nor did I ever mean to raise religious strife against the Jews, for there is no reason to be afraid of the Jews making proselytes; but since I am challenged, let me simply translate a few pages from one of the greatest historians of the Catholic Church—one who would not relate a falsehood—*l'Abbe Rohrbracher*, in the "*Historie Universelle de l'Eglise Catholique.*"

Here is what l'Abbe Rohrbracher says:—"About this time (1185) the Jews had come into evil notoriety in the West. The young King of France, Phillip Augustus, showed a great aversion for them, even though they were powerful throughout his kingdom and especially Paris. His biographer, Rigord, tells the reason—"This prince was often heard to say to the noblemen who had been brought up with him at court that every year on Holy Saturday or another day in Holy Week, the Jews of Paris out of contempt for the Christian religion used to murder a Christian, as if in sacrifice, in the underground places of the city. A they had continued for a long time in this diabolical hatred they were convicted many times during the lifetime of his father, and had been burnt at the stake for their crimes. Moreover, the Jews had killed and crucified St Richard." So speaks Rigord in his life of Phillip Augustine. This is also confirmed by William, of Aremorica, another chaplain of the same king. Another contemporary Robert, Abbe of Mount St Michael, bears witness to the same statistics under the year 1171. Thibaut, Count of Chartres, he says, burnt several Jews living at Blois, because after having crucified a child at Easter out of hatred to the Christians, they had put it into a sack and thrown it into the Loire where it was afterwards found. The Jews convicted of this crime were delivered to the flames, except those who embraced the Christian faith. They did the same cruelty to St William at Norwich in England, in the time of King Stephen. The martyr's body was interred in the Cathedral Church and miracles were wrought at his tomb. There is mention, too, of a similar case at Gloucester, in the reign of Henry II. In France, likewise, the impious Jews have done the same, in the Castle of Pontoise, to St Richard, whose body having been carried to Paris and interred in the Church, became famous for the splendour and multitude of his miracles. Brompton, an English writer, records the martyrdom of the young St William in the ninth year of King Stephen's reign—which is the year 1144—that of the child crucified at Gloucester in the 6th year of Henry II—that is 1160. And lastly, we find in the chronicles of Gerald, an Englishman, and in the Annals of the Abbey of Melrose that a child named Robert was killed by the Jews at Easter, 1181, and buried in the Church of St Edmund, where, they say, he worked numberless miracles. Such, then, is the united testimony of writers, French and English, recording the history to those times. In modern days the Jews and others pretend that these facts are calumnies; but according to the historians of that epoch the Jews were convicted judicially before the Tribunals. If you say "the witnesses and judges are liars," that is no answer, for every criminal might say the same. If you say, as some say nowadays, "the Jews could not commit such crimes because God's law, which they profess, forbids such crimes"—that is to suppose a man cannot break God's law nor be a criminal. But that is begging the question. Above the Divine Law, above the Bible, the Jew puts a human law—the Rabbinical Law—The Talmud. Now, the Talmud not only permits but commands the Jew and recommends him to deceive and to kill a Christian every time occasion offers. This is a fact beyond doubt, and merits the concentrated attention of peoples and kings. Sixtus of Sierra—a Jewish convict of the 16th century—in his "Bibliotheque Sainte" selects parts of the Talmud, from which he takes the following passages.—

1—We ordain that every Jew curse three times a day all the Christian people, and pray God to confound them and exterminate them with their Kings and Princes; and that the priests do so, especially while praying in the Synagogue, in hatred of Jesus the Nazarene.

2—God gives permission to the Jews to appropriate to themselves the goods of the Christians as often as they can—be it by fraud, or violence, or usury or theft.

3—All Jews are ordered to look on all Christians as brutes, and not to treat them better than the animals.

4—Jews can do no harm, nor can the Gentiles do any good; they shall, for this reason, strive by every means to kill the Christians.

5—If a Jew, wishing to kill a Christian, kill a Jew by mistake, he deserves pardon.

6—Should a Jew see a Christian on the edge of a precipice, he is bound there and then to throw him over.

A converted Rabbi of our own times attests the same in other words.

—Rohrbacher (Bk lxx pp 405-407)."

In the second half of the 15th century the Church had the glory of more than one martyr sent to Heaven. The first was a young child. St Andrew was born November 16th, 1459, near Innsbruck in the Tyrol. Having lost his father at an early age, he was reared by his godfather who lived in a house near the Bolsano main road. As Andrew was playing one day in company with other children, he was seen by a party of Jews who were taken with the boy's appearance. These wicked-minded individuals asked the godfather to give them the child that they might look after his education. At the same time they offered a substantial bribe in the shape of a large sum of silver. They were ten in number and were headed by a Rabbi. Having become the owner of Andrew, they took him into a wood, placed him on a large stone and circumcised him, uttering at the same time most horrible blasphemies against the Holy Mass of Jesus. The boy begged for mercy, but they then took him, opened his veins, fastened him in the form of a cross to a tree and ran away. When news of this tragic occurrence was raised abroad they tried to hide the remains of the unfortunate child and buried them at Rinn, when God attested the holiness of the young martyr by a multitude of favours granted to a concourse of Christians. From that hour the tomb of the blessed Andrew was visited by pilgrims from all the neighbouring countries and even from several parts of France. The Emperor Maximilian built a chapel on the spot." These extracts speak for themselves, and if Mr Davitt is able to disprove these historical statements of the Abbe Rohrbacher, from whom I am simply translating, let him. But I do not want to treat this as a religious question, as I hear said,—my sole reason for speaking was because of the usurous trade that the Jews are carrying on in our midst. Their method of trade is nothing new—here is an extract from Pastor's History of the Popes. Speaking of usury, he says:—In the latter half of the fifteenth century, it was the Franciscans, who, with the sanction of the Apostolic See, took this social reform in hand. Intercourse with all classes of society had rendered them familiar with the pitiless greed with which Jewish and Christian money lenders took advantage of a temporary embarrassment to demand incredible high interest. To prevent the extortionate trading upon the need of the smaller towns-folk, the Franciscans resolved to found institutions where any one in need of ready money could obtain it in exchange for some pledge and without interest, the working capital of the scheme being supplied by voluntary contributors, collections, gifts, legacies, hence the expression, mons (mountain) meaning a heap of money, the owner of which was supposed to be the poor in general, or the institution. The Pope at once recognised the importance of these establishments, and encouraged them to the utmost of their power. S Bernardino da Feltre especially was indefatigable in this direction. The extraordinary rapid diffusion of these institutions is the best proof that they responded to a real want especially in the smaller towns. They met also with plenty of resistance. The war that was carried on against them is significant as a proof of the predominance and social power, which, through the control of the exchange, the Jews had acquired in Italy at the time. In Saint Bernardino's unwearied and unspairing denunciation of the Jews we are led to see what a baneful influence they excercised throughout the whole of Italy, and how they drained the life-blood of the people both rich and poor. The result was a wide spread anti-semitic movement, which sometimes led to reprehensible excesses. Saint Bernardino must not be held responsible for these, for he denounced the Christsan usurers as well as the Jews, and deprecated all violence. "No one," he said, in his sermon at Crema, "who values the salvation of his soul will dare to injure the Jews, either in their person or their property, or in any other way. For we owe Justice and Christian charity to all men, and the ordinances of the Popes and the spirit of Christianity alike enjoin this, but on the other hand the Church forbids us to maintain intimate relations with the Jews." Nevertheless some Jewish usurers endeavoured to procure his assassination. At Modena a Jewess sent him some poisoned fruit. St. Bernardino escaped and continued his labours. In 1486 Innocent VIII. called him to Rome, and soon after a Bill in favour of the Monte was issued."—History of the Popes by Pastor.

Mr Davitt complains that I, in a spirit of pretended zeal, endeavoured "to stir up a spirit of barbarous malignity." I will let you, my brothers, say whether or not my zeal is pretended. It can hardly be pretended zeal to work here day after day without one day's holiday in the year, without an hour's rest during the day, and even during the short hours allowed for sleep by our rule—to work during these hours for you. But let God alone Judge the priest's zeal. Mr Davitt again proceeds:—

"I protest as an Irishman and as a Catholic against this spirit of barbarous malignity being introduced into Ireland, under the pretended form of a material regard for the welfare of our workers. The reverend gentleman complained of the rags and poverty of the children of Limerick, as compared with the prosperity of the Jews, and on this ground deliberately incited the people of that city to hunt the Jews from their midst."

THESE WORDS OF SARCASM

on the rags and poverty of our people have an unexpected sound in the mouth of Mr Davitt It does not become him to laugh at Irish poverty. Nor have I deliberately "incited the people to hunt the Jews." My words were and are—"Have nothing to do with the Jews. If you have transactions with them, get out of them as soon as you can, then keep away from them."

Mr Davitt again says:—

"Let me suggest a field for his reforming energies which will not require the invocation of any poisonous feeling of racial animosity or of un-Christian hate. Let him attack the English rule of Ireland which levies £12,000,000 of taxes every year on our lives and industries, not to the good but to the injury of our country. Let him try and induce the people of this country to save a few millions every year out of the ten millions spent needlessly on intoxicating drink. Let him do work of this kind for the good of Limerick and the progress of Ireland, and the rags he complains of and the poverty he deplores will, if he is successful, vanish far more effectively and sooner than by preaching a cowardly vendetta of anti-Semitic prejudice.

"Fortunately Limerick is a stronghold of true Nationalist sentiment, and cannot be induced to dishonour Ireland by any response to such unworthy and un-Catholic invitations.

"MICHAEL DAVITT."

Let me thank Mr Davitt for his kindness in pointing out such a noble field of work, but, Mr Davitt was in daily and hourly touch with the people here as I am—if he were to see the curse brought upon the poor by the Jewish trade, if he were to see the robbery that is going on by the weekly instalment system of the Jews, and the exorbitant prices demanded for wretched goods, if he were to see the misery and strife caused in the household by the dealings of the woman of the house with the Jews—if he were to see the result of their enormous usury and the efforts made by the poor to release themselves when they have become entangled in the Jewish nets, he might begin to think they were as bad an evil to Ireland as landlordism and over-taxation, and he might think there was enough for me to mind without my trying to do what he and his colleagues failed to do on the floor of the British House of Commons. And as regards the drink question, you, the men of the Confraternity, know my labours to put down that evil. Yes, "fortunately Limerick is a stronghold of true National sentiments," and cannot be induced to dishonour Ireland by any response to such an unworthy and un-Catholic letter as Mr Davitt has written. Let the members of the Confraternity investigate Jewish dealings for themselves, and then if they find what I have said is true, and I am convinced that it is true, then I appeal to you not to prove false to Ireland, false to your country and false to your religion by continuing to deal with Jews. If the Jews are allowed to go on as they have been doing in a short time we will be their absolute slaves, and slavery to them is worse than the slavery to which Cromwell condemned the poor Irish who were shipped to the Barbadoes.

NOW LEAVE THE JEWS ALONE.

Remember, I warn you to do them no bodily harm. Such a thing I could never approve of. It would not be Christian-like. But keep away from them, and let them go to whatever country they came from, and not add to the evils of our state. Let Mr Davitt write what he pleases. We know our own business here, and let this self-constituted advocate of the Jews injure his country by nurturing such an evil state of things.

murder.[85] Despite Creagh's concluding advice to leave the Jews alone, his sermon was effectively an incitement to violence (document 13).

After this sermon, the local RIC feared an outbreak of general disorder, but the following day District Inspector O'Hara reported a general improvement in the situation. Although Jewish traders failed to recover instalments due to them that day, they had not been molested or followed by crowds and the police afforded them 'all possible protection'.[86] Dublin Castle authorities, in the circumstances, did not see the need to send in extra police from outside. The RIC deputy inspector general, H. Considine, advised that the police were doing everything to contain a problem which had been exacerbated by Jews 'moving about in the many lanes and back ways of the city'. The police had 'much difficulty' in preventing isolated attacks. But sending a 'large force of police in for such duty might only accentuate the feeling which has been so ill advisedly aroused'. Considine felt it was better to act as if 'nothing really serious has occurred', and to leave matters to the local police force and 'to the good sense of the people'. He concluded that 'after some little time no doubt with the assistance of the local Parish clergy ... the matter will blow over'.[87] Later, having reviewed Creagh's second sermon, Considine felt the worst of the matter had passed since:

> The Rev Gentleman's second address makes it clear that he does not counsel nor desire overt acts directed against the Jewish Community – but he did and does advocate Boycotting; not so much because they are Jews as because their methods of dealing are in his judgment injurious to the poorer classes.[88]

Shortly before Under Secretary MacDonnell reviewed the file, one of Considine's superiors (unidentified) wrote:

> This may be the commencement of a very serious business: and calls for further inquiry. … Creagh's historical and religious references may be injudicious but this account of the methods and objects of these Jews is but a … repetition of methods which Jews have practised elsewhere to the great detriment of the – and thriftless mores.

County Inspector Hayes, meanwhile, advocated a cautious approach from the police because if they were too prominent 'it will destroy their trade'.[89] O'Hara reported on 22 January that 'no further demonstrations against the Jews have taken place'. They had been 'transmitting their business without molestation for the last few days but in very many cases have been unable to recover instalments due to them'.[90] He also reported that several people had been fined between 6d and 10s 6d at petty session in Limerick that day for disorderly conduct and assaults on Jews the previous Monday (document 14). The police had, without the need for outside reinforcements, contained a dangerous situation.

ROSECUTIONS AT PETTY SESSIONS

Statement by the Bench.

At the Petty Sessions to-day, before Messrs F Hickson, R M (in the chair), Jas F Barry, ohn Clune, Poole Gabbett and Ambrose Hall, number of charges of assault and riot arising t of attacks made on Jews in the city ard. The cases appeared to excite considerle interest. There were six charges at the it of the police, and four private prosecutions. Patrick Collins, a youth, was charged by rgeant Lonergan with riotous and disorderly nduct in Nelson street last Monday.

Mr Hickson— Under what circumstances ?

The Sergeant said he saw a crowd following meone down William street, and at the time did not know who they were after; when tness got in front he saw it was a Jew; there re small boys in front throwing mud and nes, and when witness got up to Collins, the endant dropped a stone out of his hand; llins's hands were found to be full of mud.

n answer to Mr Hickson, ergeant Lonergan said the defendant's age about 15 or 16, and the cause of the riot that on Monday last the Jews went about ecting money.

District Inspector O'Hara, in reply to Mr l, said the persons attacked on Monday e Jews, and the conduct of the people, ecially in the Irishtown, was very bad. ngs had since quieted down, but the police to take the matter up and give the Jews ection.

r Clune— I may say as one of the mem- of the Confraternity present, and who d Father Creagh speak—

r Hickson— We have nothing to do with er Creagh.

r Clune— He did nothing but deprecate uct of this kind, and the magistrates ought ut an end to it.

r Hickson— I quite agree.

r Clune— If anyone wishes to follow the ce of Father Creagh they will act contra- ry to Father Creagh's intentions by using violence. One thing I remember is that er Creagh deprecated any violence to the s, and I think violence ought to be put by the bench.

Hickson— I am very glad of your opinion such as it is, Mr Clune. I quite agree you that conduct of this kind against or anybody else should be put down by magistrates.

Clune— I thoroughly agree with you.

Hall said the Jews had a very large ess, and some of the people to whom they ied goods could not get those goods from ody else He (Mr Hall) had to do with Jews, and he always found them to be t, industrious and sober people. He know one of them to be brought up for enness, and those people had a right to e their way and do their business.

Hickson— What will you do in this case ?

Hall— I would punish every one of them. must put this kind of thing down and your disapproval of it. The Jews have a o live as well as anybody else.

Clune— On Monday you said the Jews ursued. Is it not a fact that nothing curred since.

rict Inspector O'Hara said that was so, police had to protect the Jews. The r had quieted down since.

Dodds, solicitor, (intervening) said he ir cases in which he was prosecuting, rhaps the court would take them up deciding.

Hickson asked how many cases were the suit of the police.

rict Inspector O'Hara said there were

as agreed to hear all the cases before nch gave their decision.

mas Reddan was charged with being f a disorderly crowd following and ening Jews last Monday.

McCabe stated he saw the defen-

You must put this kind of thing down and mark your disapproval of it. The Jews have a right to live as well as anybody else.

Mr Clune—On Monday you said the Jews were pursued. Is it not a fact that nothing has occurred since.

District Inspector O'Hara said that was so, but the police had to protect the Jews. The disorder had quieted down since.

Mr Dodds, solicitor, (intervening) said he had four cases in which he was prosecuting, and perhaps the court would take them up before deciding.

Mr Hickson asked how many cases were there at the suit of the police.

District Inspector O'Hara said there were seven.

It was agreed to hear all the cases before the bench gave their decision.

Thomas Reddan was charged with being one of a disorderly crowd following and threatening Jews last Monday.

Constable McCabe stated he saw the defendant catch hold of two Jews and another man pulling them; witness asked what he was doing and Reddan said if the Jew went back again for his sixpence he would knock his b——y sconce off.

Mr Hall—Where was this ?

Constable McCabe—In Lower Gerald Griffin street.

Mr Hall—This is a new way to pay old debts—not to pay them at all.

Margaret Quin was next charged with forming part of a riotous and disorderly conduct in West Wateraate.

Sergeant Rogan said the defendant was one of a riotous and disorderly crowd. She called one of the Jews a dollyman.

Mr Hickson asked if she had an infant in her arms then as she had now.

The Sergeant answered in the affirmative.

Mr Hall—Will you tell us about the money you owe to the Jews.

Defendant said she did not owe them any money. There was but one Jew present.

Sergeant Rogan said there were four.

Mr Hall—She would not know a Jew as well as you.

Defendant—Anyone would know their faces —the face of a dolly man.

Mr Hall—Ladies are now admitted to the medical profession and they want to get into the bar.

Head Constable Moore — And the dock (laughter).

Mr Clune asked how the woman conducted herself.

Sergeant Rogan—Her demeanour was not very nice.

Mr Nash, solicitor—Was there a Jew there at all ?

Defendant said she did not know if the men were Jews.

Mr Hall—Would you know the face of a Jew ?

Defendant said she would. When Sergeant Rogan spoke to her all she said was " would you not turn your back and let the crowd hit the dolly man " (laughter).

Mary Lynch was summoned for a like offence.

Constable Madden said about half-past twelve o'clock on Monday he saw a Jew go into Mrs Lynche's house, but he came out very quickly; he heard the Jew told to be off, and then there was a cheer from the crowd ; the Jew then went up Garvey's Range, and at every house where he was not paid the crowd cheered.

Mr Hickson—She was only disorderly.

Lizzie Doyle was charged with disorderly conduct also on the same occasion.

The Constable said that but for the police the conduct of the crowd would be worse than what it was; Father Fitzgerald went down the range collecting dues, and his presence had a great effect on the people.

George Harte and Kate Bell were summoned by Constable Bell on a like charge. The defendants were disorderly and there was a crowd of 300 people following the Jews in the Irishtown on Monday.

Mr Clune—Would not two dogs fighting attract as big a crowd in Broad street ?

Mr Hall—Oh, not at all.

Mr Hickson—All these cases occurred about the same time.

The Constable—One will have to be adjourned.

Mr DeCourcey—Yes, the defendant gave a wrong name and could not be served.

prosecute in four cases, and he would apply for an adjournment. Before making the application, he would just like to make a short statement. It was not necessary to enter into what led up to these occurrences, for every right-minded citizen agreed they were a disgrace not only to Limerick, but Ireland. The magistrates knew the character of the Jews for honesty and industry, and, as Mr Hall said, all they wanted was to live in peace. They never did anything the citizens could find fault with, and it was a tremendous hardship that these men should be pursued and outraged in this fashion. Their feelings were so strong on the subject that the Head of the Community of the Jews was most anxious to employ counsel to come to Limerick and put their case fairly and honestly before the public. They did not see any reason why these outrages should be committed against them. Most of them were poor and it was the exception to find them rich and he could only say that if the citizens and inhabitants of Limerick were as hard working as the Jews the city would be a great deal more prosperous than what it was. The Jews paid taxes and they were entitled to the protection of the law, and he knew that every citizen of every kind of religion condemned those outrages. That was generally admitted. With the object of bringing down counsel he would suggest to have the case adjourned for a fortnight and in the meantime see what the state of feeling was. The Jews did not wish to prosecute those defendants because they believed they were misled. Whatever was the intention of the speeches delivered they had culminated in those outrages.

Mr Nash—What speeches do you refer to I don't know, but you ought to say.

Mr Dodd—It is a matter of common notoriety, and I do not wish to refer to those speeches at all. They may have been taken up wrong, but in any case the Jews are entitled to police protection to the fullest extent. With that view I ask for an adjournment.

Mr Hickson said he was sure the interests of his clients were safe in Mr Dodd's hands, the magistrates would hear the cases.

Samuel Shockett, a Jew, summoned Anne McNamara, of Mungret street, for assault on Monday last. Defendant, an aged, blind woman, had to be assisted on to the witness table by the police.

Mr Dodd, solicitor, appeared for the complainant, and asked to have an interpreter sworn, as his client had been only seven months in Limerick.

DOCUMENT 14
23 JANUARY 1904
ARTICLE IN
LIMERICK ECHO

Report on the cases concerning anti-Semitic acts heard at the petty sessions on 22 January

continued on next page

Marks Blond, Jew, having been sworn on the Old Testament, repeated to complainant the questions put by Mr Dodd.

Mr Hickson—That is not Hebrew you are speaking.

Mr Blond—It is Yiddish.

The Witness, through the interpreter, stated he was going up Mungret street on the 18th instant; he had no actual business with defendant, but went to to inquire about a customer; he went upstairs, and defendant threw a bucket of milk on him.

Defendant denied the offence; she could not understand him nor see him; she asked him had he any commands on her.

Mr Hickson—What about the can of milk ?

Defendant—I know nothing about it no more than you.

Mr Hickson—I don't think this case is under the same designation as the other cases. This occurred in the house, and is nothing but a squabble.

Mr Dodd—No doubt but a milk can was thrown at him. They had been hunted up Mungret street at the time.

Mr Clune—This is not a very outrageous case.

Mr Dodd—But it is one of the series.

Mr Hickson—This is a different thing. He went into the woman's house.

Mrs Gray, Vize's Fields, was summoned by Samuel Fine, a young Jew, for assault on the eighteenth instant.

Mr Counihan defended, and objected to the services of the interpreter, stating the prosecutor could speak English well enough.

The Witness—I don't understand English. Not much (laughter).

Mr Hickson—You speak it very well.

Mr Counihan—He knows enough to go about this city to transact business.

The witness stated in English that passing the defendants house she threw stones at him, one of which strock him on the back, and another on the neck.

Mr Counihan—Did you see her ?

The Witness—I did not see her at all. I had passed the door when I got a stroke of the stone. There was a lot of people there. Witness ran away.

Mr Hall—Did you see a stone in her hand ? I did.

Mr Counihan—He did not say that until your worship mentioned it. He objected to Blond being employed as interpreter, stating he had been convicted before the magistrates and sentenced to two months imprisonment for an assault on his father-in-law.

Mr Hickson—Surely you would not say that because a man was convicted or an assault he should not be believed on his oath ? If so, a great many people would not be believed.

Mr Counihan said he would ask that someone else be appointed as interpreter in the circumstances.

Mr Blond—As that matter has been mentioned I would wish to say— —

Mr Hickson—There is no need for speeches. It is nonsense to say that a man would not be believed, when sworn, in a case of assault.

Louis Cramer, a Jew, was then examined through the interpreter, and swore he saw defendant throwing a stone at complainant, but did not see it strike him. Witness ran away.

Mr Counihan said his instructions were that the complainant was followed by some boys, and his client said to him "run away or the boys will kill you."

Mary Mulcahy, called for the defence, said the complainant came to the house, and was told there was no money for him until next week. He remained half an hour making faces at Mrs Gray before the crowd came up. When told to go away he would not.

Mr Hall—Did he look very ugly when he made the faces?

The Witness—Well, he did (laughter).

To Mr Counihan—She saw defendant throw a stone, but the Jews went off in the opposite way.

Louis Cramer, a Jew, summoned Michael Hilton, master sweep, for assault.

Mr Nash, solicitor, defended, and also objected to an interpreter, as the man was able to speak English.

Mr Hickson—If you were in Russia only seven months, you would not be able to speak Russian.

Mr Nash—But he is able to trade in the city.

Mr Clune—How do you sell your goods when you do not understand English ?

The Witness—I can say somethings—to buy somethings (laughter).

Mr Hickson—I cannot understand him. Mr Nash might waive his objection.

Mr Nash—Very well, sir.

The witness (through the interpreter) said he knocked at the door of defendant's house ; when it was opened defendant "stuck his fist into his breast, and said, go out of here you bloody Jew "; witness did not go exactly to defendant, but to some person upstairs who was on his book.

By Mr Nash—He forgot the name of the customer ; witness met Mr Graaf who took him to the police barrack.

Mr Nash said this was a two-penny-half-penny case.

Defendant- I never struck him.

Mr Nash—If you don't conduct yourself I will put you up a chimney (laughter). Gentlemen, I appear for Michael Hilton in this case, and at the outset I wish to say that nobody deprecates more strongly than I do insult or violence being offered to the Jewish Community, and I am fully convinced that no right minded citizen would for a moment sanction or tolerate any violence being offered to them. Gentlemen in the course of his observations, Mr Dodd referred to some speech that had been made, but on my asking him he declined to state to what speech he referred or by whom it had been made. Possibly he intended some hint or reference to some lectures recently given by Father Creagh. I don't know whether he did or not, but this much I feel bound to say that I myself was personally present at each of those lectures. I heard every word that Father Creagh spoke, and from beginning to end of them he did not utter a single word which could be construed by friend or enemy, Christian or Jew, as suggesting or inciting to any violence being used towards the Jewish community. Neither was the religious element imported into it by him, and strange to say this element was brought into it only a few days ago in a letter of Mr Davitt's which appeared in the Freeman's Journal. Now, Mr Dodd in the course of his observations spoke very strongly of the outrages that had within the last week been committed upon the Jews in Limerick, and every time he said the word "outrages" he emphasized it so strongly that you could see he wished to be underlined at least three times and have any amount of notes of exclamation after it, and in fact his language was of so bombastic and grandiloquent a character, that you would imagine that the Bulgarian atrocities were nothing in comparison with the sufferings of his clients for the last few days. Gentlemen, you have heard the evidence in all the cases, and now where are all those awful outrages ? The fact is that all the cases are two-penny-half-penny trumpery trivial charges, two of them being against two old women, feeble with age, and one of them stone blind. And the other charge is against Hilton, the evidence given in this case by the complainant himself is that Hilton pushed him with his finger. On my clients part I deny that even that trivial assault was committed, and I shall give you evidence to that effect. Now, gentlemen, I shall say no more than this, that you are gentlemen of judgment and considerable experience. You know how to deal with those cases, and the case of my client I leave confidently in your hands, and I feel confident that to-day will see an end of these troubles, and that nothing more will be heard of them in Limerick.

Mr Hall—I thought Mr Davitt's letter was after the lecture ?

Mr Nash—Yes, and he introduced the religious element.

For the defence, Pat McMahon swore no assault was committed, no violence being used by defendant.

A police constable stated that when he went to Hilton with complainant, Hilton said "I did not assault him, but I do not want him coming near this house."

This concluded the cases.

Mr Hickson said the magistrates wished to know from some responsible officer of the constabulary what was the state of affairs now as regards these Jews.

Head Constable Webster said that on Monday evening a considerable number followed the Jews through the lane-ways in which they were doing their business, and that continued about two hours.

Mr Clune—Were they grown up people ?

Head Constable Webster—There were [...] boys and girls from 14 down. The following day nothing was said to the Jews, and nothing was said since. We were around on Tuesday, but there was no hostile demonstration —not a word was said against them.

Mr Barry—Since Monday ?

The Witness—Yes.

Mr Clune—Do you think it has died out now ?

The Witness—I think it has.

Mr Dodd—I may say another case occurred on Tuesday.

Mr Nash—Another outrage !

Mr Dodd—When a Jewess was caught by the hair of the head and flung down.

Mr Clune—That is not before the magistrates now.

The magistrates having consulted,

Mr Hickson said the bench regretted the scenes of disorder which had occurred in the town. They had no evidence as to the cause of the disorder, or what had given rise to it. Mr Nash had said something about speeches—the magistrates knew nothing about them, and it was not their business to go into them. All they had to do with was the peace of the town—to see that no disorder or terrorism or intimidation was practised by one class against another, and they were determined to see law and order carried out. There were two classes of cases before the court. One class related to the Jews being followed about the town and being terrorised and intimidated. That the magistrates looked upon as being much more serious than those relating to assaults in houses. The case of Shockett against McNamara was a wretched one, and they dismissed it without prejudice. They would inflict a fine on Mrs Gray, who was acknowledged by her own witness to have thrown a stone. She would be fined 10s 6d or in default fourteen days. The case against Hilton was a very slight one, and he would be fined 2s 6d. Patrick Collins was fined 5s. In the other cases, in which the Jews had been followed through the town by large hooting crowds of men and children. People might scoff at the case of a lot of children in a crowd—that it was not one of great moment, but it was a most dangerous crowd, for when children assembled and shouted and threw mud and stones then a riot occurred. The magistrates were determined to put that down. So far as the bench was concerned they were not going to treat them very severely and hoped and trusted there would be no more of these cases no matter what the cause ; if so the magistrates would deal with them very severely. In all the other cases a fine of 10s 6d would be imposed on each defendant.

The Position of the Roman Catholic Bishop of Limerick

Rabbi Levin followed Davitt's advice and sought a meeting with the Catholic bishop of Limerick, Dr Edward Thomas O'Dwyer.[91] Levin and another leader of the community, Sol Goldberg, visited the bishop's house on 19 January and were met by O'Dwyer's secretary. The bishop did not receive them himself, but asked the two men through his secretary to refrain from making any comment to the press.[92] No account of that meeting has been found in the archives of the Limerick diocese.[93] Nevertheless, the bishop's views may be inferred from the views of the priests in his personal parishes (see document 11). It is unlikely that Frs Cregan and Lee, who voiced opposition to Creagh, would have held views contrary to those of their bishop on the matter.

Rabbi Levin then made only a brief public statement on 21 January, indicating that two considerations constrained a full reply to Creagh. First, Creagh's attack was against Jews as a whole and not against the Limerick Hebrew congregation. Second, the Limerick Hebrew congregation informed Levin that it had been requested by a high authority of the Catholic Church to avoid public controversy in connection with 'this outrageous affair'.

How did Bishop O'Dwyer respond to Creagh's attack on the Jews?[94] Creagh was a member of a religious order and that made the question of disciplining him awkward for the local bishop. O'Dwyer's position was further complicated by the fact that, according to the provincial journal of the Redemptorists, a former consultor general of the order, Fr John Magnier, and the provincial, Fr Boylan, 'were with Fr Creagh on his attack on the Jews and consequently Fr Creagh continued his campaign against the Jews'.[95] (Creagh's immediate superior, the rector of Mt St Alphonsus house in Limerick, Fr Edward O'Laverty, was not mentioned.) The same source stated that 'Bishop O'Dwyer was certainly not defending the Jews, but he was offended because he was not asked beforehand about the sermons attacking the Jews'. It was further recorded that the bishop 'gave up coming to the house. He also declared that he would not come to the General Communion of the [Feast of the] Holy Family'.[96] That event took place in the autumn at the time of the annual retreat for the members of the arch-confraternity. Is it likely, therefore, that Bishop O'Dwyer refused to visit the Redemptorist house from January until the autumn? This episcopal 'boycott' might be mistakenly perceived as a weak and inadequate response but in the world of ecclesiastical diplomacy, it was a stiff and a stern rebuke to the Redemptorists.[97]

In the months that followed Creagh's sermons, the boycott of the Jews in Limerick received widespread attention in the international press, resulting in pressure from various quarters to end the conflict. There was pressure too on the leadership of the Irish hierarchy to intervene from prominent Catholic sources in England. The Duke of Norfolk asked Cardinal Michael Logue to help put an end to the boycott.[98] The president of the

London-based Jewish Board of Deputies, David Alexander, also asked the cardinal to intervene: 'The fact that we Jews have always received active sympathy from the Church to which your Eminence belongs adds poignancy to the grief with which we regard this outbreak.'[99] Logue replied to Alexander's letter 'in sympathetic terms but stated that as Limerick was outside his Ecclesiastical province he had no jurisdiction to interfere except by way of friendly suggestion'. Logue said that he was expecting to meet O'Dwyer within a few days and that he would bring Alexander's communication to O'Dwyer's attention.[100] If the two men met – and that is probable – both would have wished to see an immediate end to the boycott.

The superior general of the Redemptorists, Fr Mathias Raus, visited Limerick on 22 July 1904. Raus, who was from Alsace where traditionally there was a fairly large Jewish community, was a mild-mannered man who did his best to avoid conflict.[101] He received a warm reception when he addressed the arch-confraternity, and Creagh was loudly cheered when he thanked the congregation for the welcome given to Raus.[102] The superior general 'called upon the Bishop upon his arrival and had a long talk with him at the Palace Corbally'. It is unlikely that the meeting passed without reference to Fr Creagh.[103] Bishop O'Dwyer did not return the visit.

Raus also received an address from Rabbi Levin respectfully requesting a meeting with the superior general and his intervention to stop the boycott:

> I regret I have to say to your Excellency, that at present it is useless for a Jew to keep open his shop for any trade, for the Catholic people who were their customers will no

longer deal with them, under the mistaken idea that in so depriving us of our means of living they are complying with some religious requirement of which they would be breaking the requirements if they were to trade with us.[104]

Raus did not give Rabbi Levin an interview, but it could be argued that the superior general's visit to Bishop O'Dwyer and the Levin petition did have an impact. The *Limerick Leader* reported on 24 August 1904 that Fr Collier, formerly of Dundalk, had been appointed sub-director of the arch-confraternity. In the autumn, Bishop O'Dwyer signalled that he was prepared to visit the Redemptorist house for the General Communion of the Feast of the Holy Family but the reconciliation may not have been total.[105]

Support for
Creagh's Anti-Semitism

Whether as a consequence of the displeasure of Bishop O'Dwyer or the action of a prudent superior, Creagh was sent in February 1904 on mission to Belfast for a few weeks. Before leaving, he found that he had much popular support in Limerick. A trade union group, meeting in the Mechanics' Institute on 20 January, passed a motion that 'we fully endorse the action of the Rev. Father Creagh regarding Jews as we consider their system of trading determental [sic] to the workers of our city. We also strongly condemn the action of Mr Michael Davitt for interfering in this matter.'[106] There was a special meeting on 22 January of prefects, sub-prefects and other officials of the arch-confraternity of the Holy Family. As the *Limerick Leader* report indicated, the meeting was very supportive of Creagh and his action.

Creagh later thanked the members of the arch-confraternity, saying that they all knew his action in the matter was 'actuated by only the deepest interest for the good of the people and to direct attention to what was a great evil and one likely to cause great danger to the common good if left to go unchallenged.'[107]

While in Belfast, Creagh commented in the local press that he had no animosity against the Jews as a race:

and, as for the Jews in business, I am quite prepared to admit that there are many who are irreproachable. What

DOCUMENT 15
25 JANUARY 1904
LIMERICK LEADER
ARTICLE

Reporting on the
22 January
meeting of the
arch-confraternity
which came out in
support of Fr
Creagh

Limerick Leader 25. 1. 04

THE JEWS

ACTION BY ARCHCONFRATERNITY

We have been forwarded the following for publication:—A special meeting of Prefects, Sub-Prefects, and other officials of the Confraternity of the Holy Family was held on Friday evening, 22nd inst., at 8 p.m., to consider what action would be taken with reference to the much-talked-of Jewish question, and Mr. Davitt's letter thereon. On the proposition of Mr. James H. Roche, seconded by Mr. John Kerr, Mr. John Dundon was moved to the chair. The following resolutions were proposed and adopted unanimously:—1. Proposed by Mr. Patrick Meagher and seconded by Mr. Michael Doyle—"That we tender to Father Creagh our best thanks for his recent lectures on the ways and means of Jewish trading, and that this meeting, representing 6,000 members of the Confraternity, express their fullest confidence with his views." 2. Proposed by Mr. Arthur M'Neice, seconded by Mr. Michael Hickey—"That we condemn the tone of Mr. Davitt's letter, and that we are of opinion our Spiritual Director, Father Creagh, was actuated by no motives except the good of the Confraternity and the general benefit of the workers of this city, especially as regards its poorest members, and that he was in no way actuated by any feeling of malignity to the Jews." 3. Proposed by Mr. J. H. Roche, seconded by Mr. John Kerr—"That we condemn any violence towards the Jews in this city, and this Confraternity dissociates itself from any acts of violence towards them." A vote of thanks to Mr. Dundon for presiding was proposed by Mr. James F. Barry and seconded unanimously. The meeting then terminated.

people have been pleased to call my crusade has been directed only against a class of Jewish traders who grind and oppress those who are unfortunate enough to get into their power – who exact extortionate sums under the instalment system from those who can ill afford to pay them.[108]

Creagh stated that his sole object was to safeguard 'my people from ruinous trading'. He said that he had strongly deprecated any violence and he had always used – and always would use – his influence to prevent it. He had simply asked the men of the arch-confraternity to 'have no dealings with them for their own sake'. However, he said that he was not 'the man to be frightened by threatening letters, and even if my life were really in peril through my action I should continue as I have been doing'.[109]

There is only one letter abusive of Creagh in the Redemptorist archives. A 'Galbally man and no Fenian' wrote:

> So you low cur had you nothing better to tell your people than to set them on the poor unfortunate Jews? You call yourself a minister of God. You are a minister of the Devil. You are a disgrace to the Catholic religion, you brute.[110]

Creagh, meanwhile, continued to receive many letters of support. The secretary of the British Brothers' League sent the text of a resolution passed on 27 April. It thanked Creagh:

> for the noble work he has undertaken to prevent a class of undesirable aliens who have received the hospitality of the Irish race from demoralising the nation and bringing misery into the homes of our Irish Brothers and Sisters through their inborn instinct of greed, usury and arrogance.[111]

A letter from 'Milesian' in the *London Times* spoke about 'an invasion of low-class Polish and Russian Jews'. The feeling in the country had turned against the Jews 'but it is chiefly against their usury and extortion'.[112] Arthur Griffith's *United Irishman* commented that its sympathy went out to:

> our countrymen the artisan whom the Jew deprives of the means of livelihood, to our countrymen the trader whom he ruins in business by unscrupulous methods, to our

countrymen the farmer whom he draws into his usurer's toils and drives to the workhouse or across the water. In short, our sympathy is so much drained by that dreary weekly procession of our own flesh and blood out of Ireland that we have none left to bestow on the weekly procession of aliens coming in.[113]

Commenting in 1904, the *United Irishman* noted that whereas twenty years before there were very few Jews in Ireland, it now argued that:

today there are Jewish magistrates to teach us respect for the glorious constitution under which we exist; Jewish lawyers to look after our affairs, and Jewish money lenders to accommodate us; Jewish tailors to clothe us; Jewish photographers to take our picture; Jewish brokers to furnish our homes, and Jewish auctioneers to sell us up in the end for the benefit of all our other Jewish benefactors. We are told the Jews are industrious people, and deserve to prosper. We do not object to their prospering by industry. We object to their prospering by usury and fraud. We object to their being given unfair advantages over the people whom they enter into competition with.[114]

The article ended:

We are glad Father Creagh has given the advice he did. We trust he will continue to give it. We have no quarrel with the Jews' religion; but all the howling of journalistic hacks and the balderdash of uninformed sentimentalists will not make us, nor should it make any honest man, cease to expose knavery, because the knavery is carried on by Jews.[115]

The *United Irishman* had already asked: 'And what greater "persecution" could be inflicted upon the Jew than to prohibit him taking his pound of flesh – with interest, three pounds.'[116] Inside, the paper protested that it did not object to the Jew seeking an honest livelihood in Ireland but 'we object to his seeking a dishonest one, and howling out that he is being martyred for his faith when the people object to him putting his hand in their pockets'. The *United Irishman* then raised the emotional issue of emigration:

> No thoughtful Irishman or woman can view without apprehension the continuous influx of Jews into Ireland and the continuous efflux of the native population. The stalwart men and bright-eyed women of our race pass from our land in a never-ending stream, and in their place we are getting strange people, alien to us in thought, alien to us in sympathy, from Russia, Poland, Germany, and Austria – people who come to live amongst us, but who never become of us. When fifteen hundred of our strong men and good women sail on the liner from the Cove of Cork, we can count on receiving a couple of hundred Jews to fill their places by the next North Wall boat. But has Ireland gained or lost by the exchange?[117]

A letter from Jacob I. Jaffe, a member of the Jewish community, appeared in the *Jewish Chronicle*:

> I know that the utterances of Father Creagh do not voice the sentiments of Irishmen in general. But – and herein the danger lies – there exists in many parts of Ireland, especially in the South and West, a class of people who, brought up in the chains of Catholicism, and trained to unquestioning and unreasoning obedience to all the dicta of their priests, need but a slight stimulus to excite them, and to rouse them from their erstwhile friendly attitude to one of defiance and frenzied hostility.[118]

The sentiments of moderate 'Irishmen in general' were reflected in the nationalist *Freeman's Journal* and in the unionist *Irish Times*.[119] But while public opinion may have reduced the level of intimidation in the city, it did not stop the boycott.

The Boycott Continues

Throughout February and March, as the boycott continued Jewish traders could not sell their goods and,
in some cases, they were not served in shops. Jewish children were ostracised in the schools.[120] The RIC county
inspector, Thomas Hayes, reported that he had visited
some members of the Jewish community on 27 January
and 'encouraged them to hold out', telling them that
'the matter would blow over – probably'. He stated that
'the Police are affording all the protection they [the
Jews] desire. It is rather a difficult matter because if the
Police are too prominent it will destroy their trade. They
are quite satisfied that what is being done is ample.'[121] In
the subdistrict of William Street, police acted upon a
series of allegations made by members of the Jewish
community. On 30 January they dealt with an alleged
refusal to supply groceries to Mr Miessel by Mr Egan.
District Inspector O'Hara had investigated immediately
and was assured by Mr Egan that he was quite willing to
supply Jews and that his shop assistant told Mr Miessel
that the groceries could not be delivered. 'The Jew being
told this was offended and went across the street to
Quinn and Co. and was supplied there.'[122] The same day
the police investigated an allegation that a member of
the Jewish community, who had bought milk from James
Gleeson of Kilpeacon, was no longer getting his supply:
'Gleeson assigned no reason to the Jew, but there was no
scarcity of milk among the Jews as a farmer named
Clancy supplied them.'[123] The police also investigated a

*Report on court
proceedings at
which Patrick
Sheehan was
charged with
assaulting a
Jewish man, Mr
Recusson*

CHARGE OF ASSAULTING A JEW.

CROSS-CASE BY DEFENDANT.

At the Petty Sessions yesterday, before Mr. Hickson, R.M (presiding), Ald: P. McDonnell, and Mr. Poole Gabbett, a young man named Patrick Sheehan was prosecuted at the suit of the police for assaulting Samuel Recusson, Colooney-street, a Jew, on the 17th March.

District Inspector O'Hara appeared to prosecute; and Mr. W. E. Counihan for the defendant.

Sheehan had a cross-case against Recusson for assault, and in this case Mr. Dodds, solicitor, appeared for the latter.

Samuel Recusson deposed that while passing the corner of the Military road and Colooney-street on St. Patrick's Day, defendant met him and caught him by the hand and said—"Why don't you leave me the milk"? He called witness "a bloody Jew," and that he ought to kill him. He then struck witness with his clenched fist on the face and also butted him with his head. after which he ran away. Witness followed him and made a complaint to the Dock police. Witness was cut in the face and was bleeding—he was treated by Dr. Myles. He had some dealings with defendant's mother, who was "a decent woman." (laughter), but stopped the milk supply because she owed him some money.

Cross-examined by Mr. Counihan—The defendant was not joking when he caught him. Denied striking the defendant; witness never struck anybody in his life. He was a long number of years in Limerick, and all he wanted was to be allowed to make a living.

Joseph Bunkin stated he witnessed the assault. He was about 40 yards away, and saw Sheehan strike the other with his fist, and also with his head in the face.

Sergeant Bockett deposed to Recusson coming to him on the day in question, and complaining to him of being assaulted. He was bleeding pretty freely from the nose, had a cut on the bridge of his nose, and his eyes were slightly blackened. Witness went to defendant's house, and after being cautioned, Sheehan admitted having struck the Jew, but denied striking him with his head.

The cross-case was then gone into.

Patrick Sheehan deposed he met Recusson on St. Patrick's Day, and commenced joking with him. The Jew gave him a box on the ear and knocked off his hat, and in picking it up his head accidentally struck the Jew in the face—he did not intentionally strike him.

Replying to Mr. Dodds, witness said he had no ill-feeling towards the Jew.

Patrick Carmody stated he saw the two men arguing, but did not see Sheehan strike the Jew.

Wm. Rainsford stated he saw the occurrence. He swore the Jew first struck Sheehan on the side of the head and knocked his hat off. Sheehan striking the Jew with his head was an accident as stated.

To Mr. Dodds—He did not see the Jew knocked down—he sat down (laughter).

Mr. Dodds said he was sorry to say that some people had not taken to heart the strong observations made from the bench on the last occasion they appeared there—

Mr. Counihan objected. This was a tirade against the people of Limerick.

Mr. Hickson—Order, order.

Mr. Dodds said these people (the Jews) were suffering under terrible hardships at the present time. Their trade was injuriously affected, and the present was but an isolated case of the kind——

Mr. Counihan—I object to this. This is a tirade which can have no effect except the creating of further bad feeling amongst the people.

Mr. Dodds said this was only an isolated case. There were a number of other assaults, which however, the people affected could not bring before the Court. He would ask the Bench to mark their sense of the injury inflicted on these men by the penalty they would inflict in the present case.

Mr. Counihan produced a character from Messrs. Shaw and Sons, where Sheehan was employed for a period of nine years.

Mr. Hickson said the assault was an unprovoked one, and were it not for the high character given by Mr. Shaw, they would send Sheehan to gaol without the option of a fine. Defendant would find it expensive to beat the Jews or to beat the police. He would be fined 20s. and costs. The cross case would be dismissed with 10s. 6d costs against Sheehan.

complaint by Rabbi Levin that 'two of his community had been ill used at Newport' in County Tipperary. On 15 February, police investigated a complaint from Ephraim Goldman that he had been stoned while passing Bank Place. On 10 March a Mr Ginsberg complained that his house was being watched by two men. That proved groundless. On 25 March, Patrick Sheehan was fined £1 and costs for assaulting Mr Recusson on 18 March.[124] The *Limerick Chronicle* reported the case and the attempt by Sheehan to bring a case against Recusson (see document 16).

There was also evidence of intimidation of Jews in rural areas. Isaac Sandler of 67 Henry Street was selling out of a car at Foynes, in the Shanagolden area, in mid-March. He had just completed the sale of two blankets to Norah Keeffe, Kilbradran, when the parish priest of Kilcolman and Coolcappa, Fr James Gleeson, drove up. What ensued was an altercation between Gleeson and Sandler and is best seen in the light of the police statements and reports (document 17).

Constable McEvoy reported to Dublin on 30 March 1904 that 'this priest's action is beyond anything I have yet had to encounter. Those Jews are examples of sobriety, industry and good conduct. They never break the law.'[125] McEvoy indicated that he was going out to the district but 'would take no action without direction'.[126] He did not interview the priest concerned.

When the matter was discussed in Dublin Castle, the RIC deputy inspector general, H. Considine, took a pragmatic view. He minuted on 8 April: 'This is a regrettable incident and I trust it will prove exceptional – but a prosecution even if sustainable (which is very doubtful) would unquestionably do infinitely more harm to the Jews than anything else.'[127] Another minute, dated 9 April, read: 'A police prosecution would be absurd.' No action was taken against the priest.[128]

DOCUMENT 17A
ISAAC SANDLER
STATEMENT

Sandler's version of his altercation with Fr Gleeson in which he claims that Gleeson told him that 'this is my parish and to clear out of it at once'

Statement of Isaac Sandler, 67 Henry St.

I was engaged selling my goods on the 15th inst at Tynes, within two miles of Shanagolden. I was after selling to Miss Keeffe, daughter of Thomas Keeffe, a pair of blankets. I had just come out of her house and I was standing on the road at my car when Father Gleeson P. P. drove up; when he saw my car he pulled up, and came off his car, and asked me "what I had sold her". I said "a little not much". He then said something to the girl about buying goods from my equals. He persuaded the girl to give back what she had bought from me. She then gave me back the blankets and said "he, the priest, would not let me keep them". He said to me "this is my parish and to clear out of it at once".

Statement of Norah Keeffe Kilbredron

I remember the Tuesday before St Patrick's day, 15 Mar 04
I was after buying a pair of blankets from a travelling
Jew. (I don't know his name) I had the blankets brought
into the house, the Jew had a car outside. immediately
after bringing in the blankets Fr Gleeson, Kilcolman,
drove up and came in here to me and said.

"I will get you out of the parish for dealing with the
"Jews and be sure and be gone out of it before a week
"and to give out the blankets which you have bought
"from him at once". I then took out the blankets
the minute he told me. I don't remember him saying
anything else to me. He (Fr Gleeson) then went as
far as the door and told the Jew to clear off the road
and that he would make him keep clear out of his
parish. The Jew said he did not care about him
nor his parish

Mrs Norah Harrington was with me when
I was buying the blankets but when she saw
Fr Gleeson coming on she ran into an outhouse
and hid in it till the priest went away

      (sgd) Norah Keeffe

DOCUMENT 17B
NORAH KEEFFE
STATEMENT

Keeffe's version
of the altercation
in which she
claims that
Gleeson said to
her: 'I will get
you out of the
parish for dealing
with the Jews'

Statement of Isaac Sandler
a Jew of 67 Henry St.

*The constable
notes that Norah
Keeffe appeared
'to resent Fr
Gleeson's
interference in
such a manner'*

County of Limerick

Shanagolden 29 March 1904

I beg to state that I enquired
of Miss Norah Keeffe, Kilbreedron,
today regarding this occurrence.
and as she made no secret or denial
of what she alleges took place I
took a statement from her a copy
of which I attach. I also went to
the woman, Norah Harrington, referred
to in Miss Keeffes statement, but Mrs
Harrington denied having heard any
of the conversation between Fr Gleeson
and the parties but admits having
ran away and concealed herself in
an outhouse when she saw Fr Gleeson
coming on.

This Norah Keeffe appears very
frank in her version of the occurrence and
appears also to resent Fr Gleesons interference in such a manner. She is a
poor herdsman's daughter and says only
for the Jews that a good many of her class
would be often in a bad way for
clothing and bed covering.

Fr Gleeson is Parish Priest of

74

Kilcolman and Coolcappa.

I have not gone to him or made any further inquiries at present.

Wm "M'Croy
Serg 46004

Rathkeale
30 , 3, '04

Submitted ,

This priest's action is beyond anything I have yet had to - on counter, those Jews as examples of sobriety, industry, & good conduct, They never tell of the law I am going out there but will of course take no action without direction

DOCUMENT 17E
POLICE REPORTS
6 APRIL 1904

RIC
constabulary
update on
the
Sandler–Gleeson
situation in which
he says that
Sandler could 'do
no trade there [in
Shanagolden]'
and that his trade
was 'in ruins in
that district'

It appears that Sandler was out in Father Gleeson's parish this week, and that nothing unusual occurred.

Wm Beckett
Sergt 46733

Limerick 6. 4. '04

Submitted. 1

Kept this file in order to see Sandler but he is still away. I saw his brother, however, to-day who told me he himself had been in Shanagolden yesterday & that he could do no trade there. A man, whom he believes to be Norah Keeffe's father, told him not to come near the house again & he says his trade is ruined in that district.

He expressed his opinion that the police should prosecute Fr. Gleeson for intimidation & said if they did not he would but that they should do it.

Pressure to Prosecute
Fr Creagh

There had been pressure also to prosecute Fr Creagh, which the police recommended against, deeming such an action likely to do more harm than good. In late January the London Committee of Deputies of British Jews petitioned the chief secretary of Ireland, George Wyndham, to take action against Creagh but it was felt such action would aggravate matters (documents 18 and 19).

Dublin Castle essentially took its advice on this matter from the police and was guided by their interpretation of events on the ground. On 30 January, District Inspector O'Hara recommended against prosecuting Creagh, and this influenced Inspector General Considine's recommendation to the under secretary (documents 20 and 21).

The London committee sent another letter on 5 April, claiming that twenty of the thirty-five Jewish families in Limerick were stated to be now ruined and compelled to beg for a bare sustenance. It was further claimed that no member of the community was able to step out of doors without risk of bodily injury (document 22).

The reply from Dublin Castle pointed out that the lord lieutenant had earlier directed the police force to 'afford every protection to the members of the Jewish faith' in Limerick and he was 'satisfied that these instructions have been fully carried out' (document 23).

Both the local police and Dublin Castle officials re-acted negatively to correspondence in the press which painted – as they perceived it – a distorted and exag-gerated view of the situation of the Jews in Limerick. On 1 April 1904, the director of the Irish Mission to Jews, I. Julian Grande, wrote to the *Irish Times*, the *London Times* and the *Express* outlining the reality of the boycott, provoking an editorial in the *Daily Express* the same day (documents 24 to 26).

The *Daily Express* continued to cover the Limerick developments, and in a manner that cast the people in a bad light, such as when they reprinted letters and articles from the *Jewish Chronicle* on 9 April, and the *Northern Whig* published a letter from Grande on 12 April detail-ing the deplorable plight of the Jews in 'lawless' Limerick (see documents 27 and 28).

The police reacted immediately to the allegations Grande made on 1 April that the police offered only 'passive protection'. Anxious to counter the suggestion that mere 'passive' police protection had been afforded the Jews, Sergeant Moore of William Street Police sub-district reported some inaccuracies in Grande's letter (document 29).

William Street subdistrict also compiled a list of com-plaints made by the Jewish community and action taken by the police (see document 30).

District Inspector O'Hara reacted to the allegations made by Grande and the *Daily Express*. In reports on 7 and 8 April he stated that Jewish business in the city was 'almost at a standstill', but took issue with criticisms of police action (see documents 31 to 32).

Deputy Inspector General Considine supported the

line taken by the police throughout, adding, in a minute on 9 April, 'That these people should suffer is earnestly a matter for regret to every one.' However, he insisted that the police 'have done, are doing, and will continue to do all they can to prevent any illegal interference with the members of the Jewish Community'.[129] And he disagreed with the *Daily Express*' claim that the 'only offence of the Jews is that they belong to a different creed', as he believed that 'the methods of doing business practised by the Jews are entirely responsible for the agitation'.[130] O'Hara repeated that point in a report on 13 April, in which he emphasised that it was the Jewish trading system, not religion, that was rejected by Creagh (see document 33).

In Dublin Castle, Considine minuted the under secretary saying that O'Hara might be correct in his view that Creagh wished to attack the Jewish system of trading and was actuated by no feeling of religious rancour. Considine himself had his reservations about the system but 'the Rev. Gentleman [had] selected both an unfortunate method and an unfortunate time.[131] The Considine interpretation, itself influenced by O'Hara's reports, essentially informed policy in Dublin Castle. When the chief secretary for Ireland, George Wyndham, faced a question on Limerick in the House of Commons on 14 April, he was briefed by Under Secretary MacDonnell, who reiterated the police line (document 34).

MacDonnell's reply had been noncommittal on whether Creagh's sermon had been brought to the attention of the Catholic bishop, and the chief secretary in London was able to cable Dublin and get a reply before going to the Commons to answer the parliamentary

DOCUMENT 18
24 JANUARY 1904

Letter in which the
London
Committee of
Deputies of British
Jews 'earnestly
and respectfully
asks that the public
prosecution of Fr
Creagh may be
ordered'

following two pages

question (document 35). The use of the telegram allowed Dublin Castle to monitor events from afar, but remain up to speed with developments on the ground through O'Hara's near daily updates.

Then, when asked by Thomas Sloan (Belfast South) whether he would order an enquiry into the whole matter in order to protect the rights of Jews, Wyndham was well equipped to reply, taking care, however, not to answer an incidental question raised by the Limerick MP, Joyce, who asked whether there was any intention to introduce legislation to safeguard against 'extortional usurers' (document 36).

Sir,

I am directed by my Board which has for the last 150 years been the representative body of the Jews of the United Kingdom, to thank you for your prompt action in taking steps to ensure that the Jews of Limerick should receive Police protection against the organised attack recently made upon them — the subject of my Board's telegram to the Under-Secretary of State for Ireland of the 19th instant.

Unfortunately the outbreak has a far more serious aspect which will not be remedied by light fines imposed on a few of the rioters.

The inflamatory and slanderous speech by Father Creagh of Limerick delivered by him at the weekly meeting of the Arch-Confraternity of the Holy Trinity on January 11th, is alone responsible for the outbreak and ill feeling against the local Jews, and I enclose a paper cutting of this speech for your perusal. Although the meeting was ostensibly only open to members of the Confraternity yet full and verbatim reports were printed in the Local Press and it is obvious that the speech was intended to have a general circulation.

It is hardly possible to imagine an attack of a more revolting nature or one more likely to inflame the minds of the audience and to lead to a breach of the peace, and the personal injury done to individual Jews by the Catholics of Limerick was a natural consequence of the speech.

The main object however of Father Creagh is to make the position of the Jews of Limerick so intolerable as to force them to leave the district, and it is unfortunately but too evident that his mendacious statements are producing the effect which he desires. Not content with his first speech, he made a second one on Monday January 18th which is even more offensive than the first, and contains perhaps the grossest insult to the Jewish religion which has been offered in any civilized Country within the memory of my Board.

A press report of the second speech is also enclosed —

My Board is informed that these speeches are with...

My Board is informed that these speeches are intended to be followed by others at short intervals, presumably until every one of our Co-religionists shall have been driven out of the town —

The statements in Father Creagh's speeches are of so extraordinary and mythical a character that were they addressed to an educated audience they would defeat their own end — But the Jews of Limerick are for the most part small traders, and, as such, are dependent for their livelihood on the goodwill of their Customers among the lower classes; and the statements of Father Creagh have gained such credence among the latter that the boycott so emphatically demanded in his speeches is already an established fact. My Board learns, on reliable authority, that Jewish trade is entirely at a standstill and that the Jews themselves have nothing to look forward to, but ruin, unless immediate steps are taken on their behalf.

Nor is the evil likely to be limited to Limerick. There is good ground to believe that unless stern measures are promptly taken to punish the instigator, the boycott will extend to other districts in Ireland where Jews reside in small numbers.

My Board feels that His Majesty's Government cannot but view with displeasure the successful endeavours of Father Creagh to render the position of the Jews an impossible one in his district and so to revive the persecutions of the middle ages — My Board therefore earnestly and respectfully asks that the public prosecution of Father Creagh may be ordered and that in the meantime he may be restrained from further inflaming popular prejudice against the local Jews —

Commending this application to your early and sympathetic consideration

I am,
Your Obedt. Servt.

Letter to
The Secretary,
London Committee of Deputies
of the British Jews,
19 Finsbury Circus,
London, E.C.

Sir,

In reply to your letter of the
25th ultimo, on the subject of recent
disturbances in the City of Limerick,
I am directed by the Lord Lieutenant
to say, with reference to the suggestion that Government should institute
a prosecution, that however reprehensible the language attributed to the
Rev. Mr. Creagh may be, His Excellency
is advised that there is not evidence
sufficient to justify the institution
of legal proceedings.   Even if it
were otherwise, it would be undesirable
to take any steps now that would tend
to revive the excitement against the
Jews in Limerick which is happily
subsiding, or that might subject them
to further injury or ill-treatment.

His Excellency rejoices to learn
that recent reports show an uninterrupted improvement in the unfortunate
and regrettable condition of affairs,
and has caused the Police Force in
Limerick to be instructed to use every
exertion to afford the fullest protection to the members of the Jewish
faith resident there.

DOCUMENT 19
REPLY TO
LONDON
COMMITTEE OF
DEPUTIES'
LETTER

*The letter states
that 'there is not
evidence
sufficient to
justify the
institution of
legal proceedings'
and that 'recent
reports show an
… improvement
[in the situation]'*

DOCUMENT 20
30 JANUARY 1904

O'Hara states that
in his opinion there
was 'no evidence
to sustain a
prosecution'
against Fr Creagh

continued on next page

I beg to
report that there is, in
my opinion, no evidence to
sustain a prosecution against
Fr. Creagh. Such a prosecution
would do more harm, if
instituted, to the Jewish cause
not merely here but all
over Ireland, than appears
to be realized by the advisers
of the Jews. The address
delivered by Fr. Creagh to
the members of the
Confraternity of the Holy Family
was in the nature of a sermon
as was delivered in the
Redemptorist church.

Possibly, had the press
not published Fr. Creagh's
remarks, so much notice
would not have been
taken of it.

No interference has
taken place with the Jews
since my last report. The

84

of them has reported that a man who used to supply him with milk has ceased to do so since the agitation began & I am investigating the matter.

Prems papers $\frac{85984}{50105}$ c. 20.1.4

C Arthur 2/1.

Limerick 1: 2: 04

Submitted. I am afraid there would be considerable difficulty in proving the case against Father Creagh, & a prosecution would increase the bitterness against the Jews -

Please see a letter from the Jewish clergyman of Limerick, submitted by me on 20th ~~inst~~ ult.

J. Burges C[?].

JG.

DOCUMENT 20
1 FEBRUARY 1904
continued

Hayes' report enclosing O'Hara's recommendation in which he advises that a prosecution of Fr Creagh might only 'increase ... bitterness against the Jews'

DOCUMENT 21
(next page)
2 FEBRUARY 1904

Considine's recommendation to the under-secretary

DOCUMENT 22
(pages 87–89)
5 APRIL 1904

Second letter from the London committee in which they claim that anti-Semitic attacks have not ceased and in fact 'individual members have received further bodily harm'

3 FEB. 1904

ROYAL IRISH CONSTABULARY OFFICE,
DUBLIN CASTLE.

Administrative Division.

SUBJECT.	MINUTE
Limerick. Agitation against the Jews in Limerick. Letter from the Solicitor & Secretary of the Committee of Deputies of the British Jews, asking that Father Creagh be prosecuted &c. Licah. with 3pio	Under - Secretary Submitted. A prosecution would manifestly do more harm than good even if a conviction could be secured, & that may be regarded as practically out of the question. While it would be a very novel departure to proceed against a clergy man for observations used by him from the pulpit in his own church. In addition the I.G. entirely fails to see what evidence is available to sustain a case. A Reporter was probably present when the observations were used since the report purports to be largely verbatim, but this man would decline to give evidence as would others who were present, & though theoretically compellable witnesses it would not in practice be found possible to compel them to give evidence. How then could the case be proved? The idea may be dismissed as outside practical consideration on every ground. Keff. E. Connidine D.I.G. 2.2.04

London Committee of Deputies of the British Jews.

19, Finsbury Circus,

London, 5ᵗʰ April 1904

CHIEF SECRETARY'S
8 APR 1904

E.C.

To His Excellency
        The Lord Lieutenant
                Dublin Castle
                        Dublin

Your Excellency

    On the instructions of this Board I addressed the Chief Secretary for Ireland on the 25ᵗʰ January last on the subject of the condition of the Jews of Limerick attributed to the Speeches of the Revᵈ Mr Creagh. Your letter dated 20ᵗʰ February last in reply stated that you were advised that there was not sufficient evidence for the prosecution of the offender and you were good enough at the same time to give a re-assuring report as to the improvement which could be noted in the unhappy state of affairs which had at the time of my letter existed in Limerick.

    Unfortunately most reliable information has since been received by my Board from numerous sources that not only has the condition of the Jewish Population of Limerick shewn no improvement but that it is actually worse now than it was at the date when my previous letter was dispatched. The boycott against the Jews, which my previous letter referred to, is stated now to be complete. Not only do the people, in accordance with the preachings of the Rev Mr Creagh, refuse to do business with the Jews, but they refuse even to pay for goods delivered in the past. Of the thirty five Jewish families living in Limerick who, until the Rev: Mr Creagh commenced his attack, had been able to maintain themselves and their families adequately and independently, twenty at least, comprising over 100 souls, are stated now to be utterly ruined and have to beg for a bare sustenance, and these families were reduced to such a state of penury that a Protestant Gentleman generously came forward to relieve their immediate necessities a few days ago with a generous donation and so prevented an actual desecration of a most sacred festival.

Not satisfied with his two speeches, referred to fully in my last letter, the Rev: Mr Creagh is continuing his series of Anti-semitic attacks. As a result, not only has the ruin of a prosperous community been made more complete but its individual members have received further bodily harm. My Board learns that no Member of the Community can stir out of doors without the risk of Assault or injury. A cutting is enclosed from the Local Press relating to one of such assaults but it is rarely that the offender can be so brought to justice.

The most serious aspect of the work of this mischievous Priest, however, is the boycott which he has so successfully instituted, Irrespective of their present distress, it is impossible to conceive how these unfortunate people can earn their livelihood in the future. An application has been made that a fund for their relief should be started in London, but such a fund must necessarily be of temporary assistance, and, unless immediate steps are taken to stop the evil at its source, the whole body of Jews of Limerick, some 200 persons in all, will have to leave the City, their trade connection gone and compelled to start the battle of life afresh, many of them burdened with young families, in some other part of the Country where religious persecution does not exist.

That a persecution of this kind should be possible in any portion of the United Kingdom in modern times, and that there should be no authority superior to that of the Rev Mr Creagh to put an end to this religious intolerance is almost inconceivable. — Lest my statement of the condition of affairs may be considered as highly coloured, I am directed to enclose for your Excellency's perusal Copy of a letter dated the 30th March from the Minister of one of the Limerick Congregations of Jews and a print of a letter from a stranger and a protestant which appeared in the Times of 1st April instant, which shew that the plight of the Jews of Limerick could hardly be more intolerable. The only answer to the letter was an anonymous one in the same Journal of 4th instant in which the writer stated that the question was not a religious one but was due to the methods of trading of the Jews themselves. — It may, however, be pointed out that apart from the entire absence of proof of this charge, no objection either to the Jews or to their trading was made until the Rev. Mr Creagh commenced his scandalous series of speeches. Until his advent the Jews had lived on amicable terms with their neighbours of all creeds. Moreover the virulence of his first two speeches was obviously directed against the Jewish religion which he foully slandered. —

Your Excellency will see how urgent it is that some immediate action should be taken, not only on behalf of the actual sufferers who are at present denied the protection of life and freedom of trade, but to prevent this Priest, who is probably only just embarking on his campaign, or others of his confraternity carrying his practice into other districts in Ireland. The very fact that the Rev. Mr Creagh is permitted to take the law into his own hands and to preach violence without interference gives more weight to his preachings with his ignorant audience — It is not to be hoped that the position will be improved until he is made to feel that there is some limit to the patience of the Authorities

One thing is certain, namely, that any action which Your Excellency under the circumstances, may think advisable cannot make the position of my unfortunate Co-religionists more unbearable. Under these circumstances I am instructed to beg that your Excellency will be so good as to give this matter your most earnest and earliest attention,

I am,
Your Obedient Servant
Charles H. L. Emanuel

THE CHIEF SECRETARY'S OFFICE, IRELAND.

POLICE & CRIME DIVISION (ORDINARY.)

SUBJECT

MINUTE

[stamp: 29 APR. 1904]

Agitation against the Jews in Limerick.

Under Secretary,

I do not think he should enter into controversy with these people as to the state of Limerick, or discuss the functions of Gov. in relation to pulpit utterances or to the dealings between Jews and their customers.

Perhaps the annexed draft will serve.

J. B. D.

20. 4. 04.

Sub. to Chief Sec.
letter before
yours

seen by Chief Secretary 2.40 26/4/04
& disp. 26/4

Done 25/4/4
hr.

Note.

Seen & returned
Hy. I. Considine

Write to the Secretary, London Committee of Deputies of the British Jews :-

With further reference to your letter and enclosures of the 5th. instant, I am directed by the Lord Lieutenant to state that as you have been already informed in my letter of 20th. February last, His Excellency directed ~~instructed~~ the Police Force at Limerick to afford every protection to the members of the Jewish faith in that city. His Excellency is satisfied that these instructions have been fully carried out.

The Police have discharged their duties zealously and in several instances have succeeded in prosecuting to conviction persons whom they have found participating in acts of violence towards Jews.

His Excellency is satisfied that the Police will continue to give to the Jewish inhabitants of Limerick all the protection in their power.

J. G.
To see
J. B. D.

BOYCOTT OF JEWS IN LIMERICK.

TO THE EDITOR OF THE TIMES.

Sir,—I beg to request a little space in your valuable journal to bring before the public the serious condition of the Hebrew community in Limerick. I notice by a letter from the Lord Lieutenant of Ireland to the Jewish Board of Deputies that he assures the said board that "things have quieted down and show an "uninterrupted improvement," and that so far as His Majesty's Government is concerned it does not intend to take any measures in the matter. Sir, I have spent a whole week visiting daily the Hebrew community in Limerick, from where I have just returned, and all I can say is that their condition at present is simply appalling. The boycott is in full force; and not only do the people decline to deal with the Jews, but they even refuse to pay what is due to them for goods purchased in the past. No Jew or Jewess can walk along the streets of Limerick without being insulted or assaulted. The police give them, so far as I was able to see, passive protection. Only last Friday a man was charged with seriously assaulting a Jew in the public street of Limerick. It was proved by the Crown and admitted by the prisoner that the Jew did not offer the slightest provocation; and although the police in their evidence stated that the Jew had to be taken to a doctor to have his injuries attended to, yet the magistrates thought it sufficient merely to fine the "Catholic" prisoner 20s. Justice, however, has long since departed from lawless Limerick, and this fact was confirmed only two weeks ago by the Lord Chief Baron, who told the jury and the public that "there is no justice in Limerick."

The boycott, unfortunately, does not apply to the city of Limerick alone; for those responsible for the present trouble are not satisfied with having incited the mob in the city, but they have been sending out circulars all over the country with the most inflammatory extracts from Father Creagh's sermon telling the peasantry and others that they are not to deal with the Jews. A case of high-handed conduct on the part of an Irish priest occurred last week 20 miles distant from Limerick. A Jew pedlar called in a certain village to sell his goods. A woman had just purchased from the man a pair of blankets, and arranged to pay for them at the rate of 1s. per week, the man not receiving at the time any money. He was just about to leave the house when a car drove up and the parish priest, entering the house, met the Jew and demanded from him what he was doing there. The Jew said that he was about his ordinary business. The priest then asked the woman what she had bought, and when she pointed to the blankets which were lying on the table he took them up, threw them out through the doorway, and told the man to leave the village and never enter his parish again, at the same time remarking to the woman, "Do you not know that you must not deal with the Jews?"

Such, Sir, is the state of affairs existing at present in Limerick and that part of the country. The number of Jews in Limerick consists of 35 families. With the exception of two or three the majority of them are ruined and on the verge of starvation. Two or three Protestant gentlemen have been obliged already to give immediate relief to at least 15 families. The Jewish Rabbi told me, and I know from personal knowledge, that up to this no relief was ever required by any of the Jewish residents in Limerick. I know of the members of one family who have resided there for nearly 20 years, and the man was able to support himself and family on the 25s. per week which he earned. His children are now grown up. A son of his graduated last year in the Royal University. Yet the same man has, within the last two months, had to sell all his furniture and other personal belongings for the purpose of buying food, as since the boycott came into force he has been ruined and prevented from earning anything. The same thing applies to the majority of the other Jewish families in Limerick.

The few Protestants in Limerick can only sympathize deeply with the Jews, whom they always found to be a sober, quiet, and law-abiding community. The Protestants dare not help them openly, as they do not know when their own turn may come or when they too may find themselves at the mercy of Redemptorist priests (which, like justice in Limerick, is conspicuous by its absence).

May I, therefore, in all sincerity and earnestness, ask the Anglo-Jewish Association or other responsible members of Anglo-Jewry, and all who pity the downtrodden and persecuted Jew, to come to the assistance of the perishing and boycotted Israelites in Limerick? The matter admits of no delay; starvation and homelessness stare them in the face.

I may mention that while in Limerick I had a long interview with Father Creagh, the Roman Catholic priest, whom the Jews and others charge with being the cause of all their present misery; and after 55 minutes' talk, during which we discussed fully and freely the Jewish question in Limerick, I am convinced that while Father Creagh remains in that city directing its Roman Catholicism the Jews will have to leave, and many of them have not as many shillings in the world as would pay their fares even as far as Dublin.

THE JEWS IN LIMERICK

TO THE EDITOR OF THE IRISH TIMES.

Sir,—I beg to request a little space in the Irish Times to bring before the public the serious condition of the Hebrew community in Limerick. I notice by a letter from the Lord Lieutenant for Ireland to the Jewish Board of Deputies that he assures the Board that "things have quieted down and show an "uninterrupted improvement," and that so far as His Majesty's Government is concerned it does not intend to take any measures in the matter. Sir, I have spent a whole week visiting daily the Hebrew community in Limerick, from where I have just returned, and all I can say is that their condition at present is simply appalling. The boycott is in full force, and not only do the people decline to deal with the Jews, but they even refuse to pay what is due to them for goods purchased in the past. No Jew or Jewess can walk along the streets of Limerick without being insulted or assaulted. The police give them, so far as I was able to see, passive protection. Only last Friday a man was charged with seriously assaulting a Jew in the public street of Limerick. It was proved by the Crown, and admitted by the prisoner, that the Jew did not offer the slightest provocation, and although the police in their evidence stated that the Jew had to be taken to a doctor to have his injuries attended to, yet the magistrates thought it sufficient merely to fine the prisoner 20s. Justice, however, has long since departed from lawless Limerick, and this fact was confirmed only two weeks ago by the Lord Chief Baron, who told the jury and the public that "there is no justice in Limerick."

Such, sir, is the state of affairs existing at present in Limerick and that part of the country. The number of Jews in Limerick consists of 35 families. With the exception of two or three the majority of them are ruined, and on the verge of starvation. Two or three Protestant gentlemen have been obliged already to give immediate relief to at least 15 families. The Jewish Rabbi told me, and I know, from personal knowledge, that up to this no relief was ever required by any of the Jewish residents in Limerick. I know of the members of one family who have resided there for nearly 20 years, and the man was able to support himself and family on the 25s. per week which he earned. His children are now grown up. A son of his graduated last year in the Royal University. Yet the same man has, within the last two months, had to sell all his furniture and other personal belongings for the purpose of buying food, as, since the boycott came into force, he has been ruined and prevented from earning anything. The same thing applies to the majority of the other Jewish families in Limerick.

May I, therefore, in all sincerity and earnestness, ask the Anglo-Jewish Association or other responsible members of Anglo-Jewry, and all who pity the down-trodden and persecuted Jew, to come to the assistance of the perishing and boycotted Israelites in Limerick. The matter admits of no delay—starvation and homelessness stare them in the face.—Yours, &c.,

I. JULIAN GRANDE,
Director of "The Irish Mission to the Jews,"
43 Upper Sackville street, Dublin,
30th March, 1904.

DOCUMENT 23
(*previous page*)
APRIL 1904

Dublin Castle's reply in which they state that 'the police have discharged their duties zealously' and would continue to give the Limerick Jews 'all the protection in their power'

DOCUMENT 24
(*this page on left*)
LONDON TIMES
1 APRIL 1904

I. Julian Grande's letter to the London Times *in which he contradicts the official line of the lord lieutenant of Ireland, stating that 'the boycott is in full force'*

DOCUMENT 25 (*right*)
IRISH TIMES
1 APRIL 1904

I. Julian Grande's letter to the Irish Times *in which he states that 'No Jew … can walk along the streets of Limerick without being … assaulted'*

DOCUMENT 26 (left)
DAILY EXPRESS
1 APRIL 1904

*Editorial reacting
to I. Julian
Grande's letter in
which the writer
states that the
'shameful cruelty
[to the Jews] is the
direct outcome of
the clerical advice
not to have any
dealing with the
Jews'*

Our readers will not be greatly surprised, however much they may be shocked, at the revelation of the condition of the unhappy Jewish residents of Limerick which Mr. Julian Grande makes in the letter which we publish from him this morning. Mr. Grande has recently paid a visit to Limerick on behalf of the Irish Mission to the Jews, and he finds the majority of his compatriots absolutely destitute; a boycott against the Jews is in full swing; justice is denied to them, or at least such justice as they can secure is a mere travesty; and the only liberty which they can get in carrying on the work on which their livelihood depends is the liberty to starve or emigrate. Mr. Grande gives the facts and figures for his charges. In one case, a priest, he states, intervened between a Jew and his customer, threw the goods the latter had purchased out of the house, and ordered the Jew to leave the parish. This is toleration and Christian charity as they are understood in Limerick and its neighbourhood. Is it surprising that the Hebrew community in this district is starving? A Jewish trader, who has lived in Limerick for twenty years, and brought up a family on an income of five-and-twenty shillings a week, and put one of his sons through the Royal University of Ireland, it is also stated, has been unable to earn anything for two months, and has been compelled to sell his furniture to feed those depending upon him. There can be no doubt that this shameful cruelty is the direct outcome of the clerical advice not to have any dealing with the Jews. There are thirty-five Hebrew families in Limerick, and the majority of them, Mr. Grande tells us, are in absolute danger of starvation. The little relief that isolated Protestants can give them can only tide them over their difficulties, but cannot remove them. The authorities content themselves with the expression of pious opinions, and in the meantime the victims of religious hatred must go hungry. We say nothing of the Christianity of those who are responsible for this merciless and shameful boycott; that is a matter between themselves and their own consciences. But we do think that it is a crying scandal that the educated bigots of Limerick should be allowed to make life intolerable for law-abiding and industrious members of the community, whose only offence is that they belong to a different creed. The Lord Lieutenant has been informed that there has been an uninterrupted improvement in the condition of affairs in Limerick. We are afraid that this comforting assurance cannot adequately take the place of the daily bread that is denied the victims of Limerick race-hatred.

DOCUMENT 27 (right)
DAILY EXPRESS
9 APRIL 1904

*Sample letter to the
Express reacting to
the Jewish situation
in Limerick
reprinted from the
Jewish Chronicle*

The "Jewish Chronicle" writes:—The community will learn, with the deepest pain, of the deplorable situation existing in the city of Limerick. We had hoped that the trouble, the beginning of which we reported in January, would quickly blow over, and that peace would be restored between the different sections of the population. In that hope we were encouraged by the sympathetic letter of the Lord Lieutenant, who assured the Board of Deputies that "recent reports show an uninterrupted improvement in the unfortunate and regrettable condition of affairs." We now understand that his Excellency has been grievously misled. So far from an improvement having set in, the boycott—always a dread weapon in the experienced hands of the Irish—has been enforced with ruthless severity against the Jews. Where the peasantry have seen no cause for so inhuman a proceeding, they appear to have been egged on by priestly supporters of Father Creagh, much in the same way as the anti-Semitic ardour of the Roumanian peasantry has to be jogged occasionally by Roumanian politicians. The result of this shameful campaign is that the thirty-five Jewish families who live in the city are reduced to destitution. From self-supporting citizens they have become a crowd of beggars dependent for their bread upon the benevolence of Protestant friends, who know that, any day, the same potent weapons may be turned against their own people. Perhaps the next stage in this gloomy drama will be an agitation for the expulsion of the Limerick Jews on the ground that they are "destitute aliens." The rapidity with which these unfortunate people have become penniless scarcely suggests that their much denounced business practices have been lucrative, and it is daily more obvious that the motive at the bottom of this wicked movement was one of religious bigotry, pure and simple, coupled with the ill-feeling that seems to dog every considerable aggregation of members of the Jewish race.

Submitted.

[signature]

9. 4. 04

THE BOYCOTT OF THE JEWS IN LIMERICK.

TO THE EDITOR OF THE NORTHERN WHIG.

Sir,—May I again request a little space in your journal for the purpose of bringing before the public the condition of the persecuted and boycotted Jews in Limerick? A letter by the Rabbi of the Limerick Hebrew community, which appeared in yesterday's "Jewish Chronicle," and of which I here give an extract, will show the sad plight of these unfortunate people just now—"It is with deepest sorrow," writes the Rabbi, "I have to inform you that the condition of my poor community is deplorable. The oppression and affliction which the Redemptorist priest Creagh has brought upon us are really too heartbreaking to attempt to describe. Owing to the boycott of the Jews' trade in Limerick the majority of the thirty-five Jewish families resident here are absolutely destitute. . . . The letter from Mr. Grande (published on Good Friday) gives a clear and vivid illustration of the state of affairs of the Jews in Limerick." From this it will be seen that no change has as yet taken place in the situation. Your powerful contemporary, the "Times," in conjunction with your journal and the Press generally, has already rendered signal service to the oppressed and wronged thirty-five Hebrew families in Limerick. As a result of your kind publication of my letter on Good Friday, the latter has been the means of not only awakening the practical sympathy of Christian friends all over the country, but from directly private communications I have received this day from the heads of the Jewish people in London I am glad to say that definite action has been taken by the Law and Parliamentary Committee of the Jewish Board of Deputies. For the present, however, the boycotted people, who will remain at all costs in Limerick, no matter what their tormentors may next resort to, will have to be temporarily assisted. The Advisory Council of the Irish Mission to the Jews, which represents all the Protestant denominations in Ireland, and of which T. Pakenham Law, Esq., K.C., is the president, has established a special relief fund for the purpose, and it will see that every penny received is judiciously distributed. I hope to return to Limerick shortly, and shall personally, together with a resident Christian clergyman, inquire into every individual case before funds are distributed. So far the response from Christian people—most of them friends of our Society, whose object is to promote Christianity among the Jews in Ireland and elsewhere—have been on the whole generous. But, if we are to assist almost two hundred souls until things quiet down in lawless Limerick, and a change for the better takes place, we will require additional funds to enable us to carry on this most needed and Christlike work. I think the words of our Lord are very applicable to the present sad circumstances—"Inasmuch as ye have done it unto the least of these my brethren. (the Jews), ye have done it unto Me." Major Fielding, the honorary treasurer of our Mission, has formally acknowledged all the contributions hitherto received, and I shall be glad to receive any other donations for the relief of the Jews in Limerick.—Yours, &c.,

I. JULIAN GRANDE,
Director of the Irish Mission to the Jews.
43, Upper Sackville Street, Dublin,
April 11th, 1904.

DOCUMENT 28
NORTHERN WHIG
12 APRIL 1904

Letter from I. Julian Grande, written to bring 'before the public the condition of the … boycotted Jews': 'Owing to the boycott of the Jews' trade in Limerick the majority of … Jewish families … are absolutely destitute'

DOCUMENT 29
2 APRIL 1904

Letter from
Sergeant Moore in
which he reacts to
I. Julian Grande's
letter claiming:
'the letter is highly
coloured and in
some respects is
not in accordance
with facts'

William Street

2nd April 1904.

I beg to submit annexed newspaper cutting.

The letter is highly coloured and in some respects is not in accordance with facts.

The Jews here are not so well off as they were previous to the agitation which was raised against them but their condition is not, in any instance, "appalling". Some of them are very poor but none are in want. However, they are practically doing no business and in trade matters they are left severely alone. If this state of affairs continues — and it is likely to continue — they must either leave the City or fall into a condition

of want if they do not
get assistance from outside
sources. Some of them
have already been assisted
by a few Limerick gentlemen.

The Jewish Community
here have received more
than "passive" protection
from the Police. They
have been most actively
and successfully protected
since the first moment
that any hostility was
shown to them. The
Police have prosecuted
a large number of people
for assaults upon and
disorderly conduct in connection with the Jews
and whenever a case was
proved the Magistrates
convicted. The case
referred to by Mr Grande
is that of The King v.
Sheehan for an assault
upon a Jew called Recusson.

Th. Moore J.H.

48614

95

District of Limerick   Sub dist of William Street

Return showing complaints made by Jews and Police action taken in consequence.

DOCUMENT 30
2 APRIL 1904

Report showing the list of complaints made by the Jewish community since Fr Creagh's speech in January

continued on next two pages

Date	Nature of Complaint	Police action taken etc.
18 : 1 : 04	Mr Levin complained of conduct of people towards Jews collecting money.	Police were immediately sent to protect them on that day and on all other subsequent days when they went out collecting.
18 : 1 : 04	Assault upon a Jew named Julius Martinson.	Sergt. Lonergan was on the scene and prosecuted Patk. Collins who was fined 5/= & costs at P.S. 22/1/04. Collins was 14 years of age.
30 : 1 : 04	Alleged refusal to supply Groceries to Mr Missel, a Jew, by the Messrs Egan	Mr O'Hara D.I. and H.C. Moore at once inquired into this complaint and were assured by Mr Egan that he was quite willing to supply Jews and that his shop assistant told the Jew that the groceries could not be delivered. The Jew on being told this was offended and went across the Street to Quin & Coy. and was supplied there.
30 : 1 : 04	Alleged refusal to supply milk to a Jew named Goold	Goold complained to H.C. Moore who at once investigated the matter and found that James Gleeson of Kilpeacon who was in the habit of supplying the Jew with milk for retail purposes had ceased to do so. Gleeson assigned t Hc [...]

		do so. ... son assigned no reason to the Jew but there was no scarcity of milk among the Jews as a farmer named Clancy supplied them.
30 : 1 : '04	Alleged attack on Jews at Newport	Mr Levin complained to H. Moore that two of his community had been ill used at Newport. The Police there were at once communicated with.
15 : 2 : 04	Stone throwing at Bank Place at a Jew named Ephraim Goldman.	E. Goldman, a Jew, complained that some one had thrown out of an area in Bank Place some stones at him as he was passing. Const. Cassidy at once procured name and address of the man who was identified by the Jew but ...
10 : 3 : 04	Alleged picketing of a Jew's house.- complaint made to H. Moore by Mr Ginsberg that two men had been watching his house.	Plain clothes men were sent to watch whether there was any foundation for this complaint and it was shown to be groundless. Mr Ginsberg who seemed to be afraid thought that any person who stood near his house was watching it.
: 3 : 04	Assault on a Jew named Recusson	Complaint made to H. Moore by Recusson. The H. reported case to D.I. who ordered a _prosecution_ by the Police and at P.S. on 25:3:'04 Patrick Sheehan who assaulted Recusson was fined ...

In addition to the specific action taken in cases of complaints, the Police here – both plain clothes men and those in uniform – pay special attention at all times to Jews when they move about this Sub District. None of them reside in this Sub Dist.

Thos. Moore W. 48614.

'8. 1. 14 — A large crowd collected in John St. hooted Jews who were collecting their money others threw mud &c. at them

Six persons were prosecuted at P.S. 22.1.4 & fined for disorderly behaviour.

In several isolated cases since the police have got the names of persons who threw stones at Jews & gave them to the injured persons.

DOCUMENT 31
O'HARA'S
REPORT
7 APRIL 1904

O'Hara states that
claims that the
police were only
giving the Jews
passive protection
were 'unfounded'

99

DOCUMENT 32 (left)
O'HARA'S REPORT
8 APRIL 1904

O'Hara further reported that 'every assistance has been given to the Jews' and he had been told that they 'are not at all so badly off as they themselves make out'

DOCUMENT 33 (right)
O'HARA'S REPORT
13 APRIL 1904

O'Hara wrote that while 'the Jewish trade has fallen away hugely' that 'there is no general boycott of the Jews'

continued on next page

for suggesting the condition of the Jews in Limerick.

Mr. Levin told me today that the appeals made in the papers &c are not made at the instigation of the Jews. I pointed out to him that it was an exaggeration to say that the Jews were starving & he said that though they were not starving they were on the brink of starvation & must starve if things go on as at present.

The letters that are being written to the press about the Jews emanate chiefly from the offices of the "Irish Church Missions to the Jews" & the impression sought to be produced is that the agitation is entirely a religious one & that after the Jews are suppressed the same methods will be used against Protestants.

There is no foundation for this. Fr. Creagh, the Redemptorist who initiated the agitation by calling attention to the methods of business of the Jews, is a very charitable man & he backed up his advice to his congregation – to have no further dealings with the Jews – by referring in an indirect & injudicious manner to the past history of the Jews, but there is no religious crusade.

The result of his advice has been that the Jewish trade has fallen away largely but there is no general boycott of the Jews. Of course as the greater portion of their trade was with the poorer classes, who were tempted by the weekly payment system, & who have now deserted them the Jews must eventually suffer seriously. But I believe that if they allowed things to quiet down they would gradually recover their trade with the poorer classes who cannot pay ready money in shops.

Every protection is being afforded them by the police & in every case where they can identify persons who have assaulted them the police have prosecuted.

It is inevitable that in back streets children or corner boys will take advantage of the absence of a constable to call names or throw a stone but even such cases are not of frequent occurrence the attention of the police has been all through specially directed to preventing them.

C Hoften
2D.
C. I. n. land.

DOCUMENT 34
UNDER-
SECRETARY
MACDONNELL'S
REPORT
APRIL 1904

MacDonnell was
outlining the
position for the
chief secretary for
Ireland, George
Wyndham, who
was facing a
question on it in
the House of
Commons

DOCUMENT 35
(opposite page)
14 APRIL 1904

Telegram from the
chief secretary in
London asking
whether the
'language of …
Creagh … was
brought under the
notice of the RC
Bishop

Mr Sloan's Question
re Jews in Limerick.
The I. G reports.
[repeat A]
Ends. Under Sec-
retary's minute: —
The Rev Mr Creagh's
remarks regarding
Jews were addressed
to a Confraternity or
Association of Roman
Catholics on 11th &
12th Jany last and
were reproduced in
"Munster News" pub-
lished in Limerick
on the 13th They
must necessarily
have come immediately
under the notice of
the Bishop. On the
18th Jany Father
Creagh addressing
the same confrater-
nity said he desired
it to be thoroughly
understood that he
entirely and fully
deprecated any vio-
lence towards the
Jews. Such was never
his intention and
he felt sure his
advice in the matter
would be followed
by the people. He
then proceeded to
explain that it was
the method of the

Jews' trading to
which he was opposed,
and he concluding
by saying "Now
leave the Jews alone.
Remember I warn
you to do them no
bodily harm. Such
a thing I would
never approve of:
it would not be
Christian-like. But
keep away from them
and let them go to
whatever country
they came from and
not add to the evils
of our race" This
address was pub-
lished in "Limerick
Echo" of 19th Jany
and reproduced
substantially in the
Freeman. The Police
state that the methods
of doing business
practised by the
Jews are entirely
responsible for the
agitation. They
add that there is
no religious cru-
sade against Jews
and no general
boycott of them.

Message Received in Chief Secretary's Office.

Date 14. 4. 190

Handed in at the **Irish** Office at _____ Received here at 11 49 am

From	To
Taylor	Under Secretary

Mr Sloans Question for today Re Jews in Limerick Please say for the information of the Chief Secretary whether the Language of the Revd Mr Creagh in the beginning of the year was brought under the notice of the R. C. Bishop

Urgent

Insp: General
Reade
CFP

14. 4. 04

Under-Secretary.

No action of the sort indicated was taken by the Police. How far it might be wise or even effective is questionable, having regard to the fact that the Rev. Gentleman is not one of the Secular Clergy. He belongs to the Redemptorist Order.

Debates
14 April '04.

*Sloan and
Wyndham's debate
in the Commons
in which
Wyndham was
asked whether he
would order an
enquiry into the
persecution of the
Jews 'with the
view of protecting
the rights of these
people'*

Persecution of Jews in Limerick.

MR. SLOAN (Belfast, S.): I beg to ask the Chief Secretary to the Lord Lieutenant of Ireland if his attention has been called to the refusal to deal with and intimidation of members of the Jewish persuasion, and to the fact that in some cases violence has been used and many are at present starving by the refusal of dealers and shopkeepers to sell to them; and will he order an inquiry into the whole matter with the view of protecting the rights of these people.

THE CHIEF SECRETARY FOR IRELAND (Mr. WYNDHAM, Dover): Persons who formerly dealt with members of the Jewish faith in Limerick, in the course of trade, have ceased to deal with them, but any moneys due are being gradually paid. The police received special instructions to use every exertion to protect the Jews from acts of molestation or violence; eight such cases have been prosecuted and in two others proceedings are pending. It is not correct to say that individuals are starving; they are able to obtain supplies and necessaries in the locality. This deplorable exhibition of hostility to the Jews has formed the subject of repeated investigation on the part of the authorities, who will continue to afford every protection to the Jews in the pursuit of their lawful avocations.

MR. SLOAN: If I give the right hon. Gentleman cases where shops have refused to deal with these individuals will he have them investigated?

MR. WYNDHAM: Yes. Any information showing *prima facie* evidence of the law having been broken will be carefully considered.

MR. JOYCE (Limerick): Is there any intention to introduce legislation to safeguard the people against extortional usurers who charge 200 or 300 per cent. profit on shoddy articles.

No answer was returned.

The Case of the 'Boy Raleigh'

The temperature in the city was again raised in the middle of April when a fifteen-year-old youth, John Rahilly or Raleigh (he was reported under both names), was sentenced to a month in prison at Mountjoy, Dublin. He was among a group of boys who threw stones on 4 April at Rabbi Levin and two other members of the Jewish community as they passed by Carey's Row. One of the group was struck on the ankle by a stone thrown by Raleigh. The *Limerick Leader* on 15 April described how the youth cried bitterly as he was taken from the court (see document 37).

In a long editorial the same day, the *Limerick Leader* said the sentence was 'extremely harsh' and regretted that there 'was not a single Catholic magistrate at the hearing of the case' (document 38).

Meanwhile, other media reported quite differently than the local papers. On 16 April the *Northern Whig* ran an article on 'Jew-baiting in Limerick' (document 39), while the *Weekly Northern Whig* reproduced a letter that Julian Grande had written to the *Times* in response to one of its correspondents, 'Milesian' (document 40).

District Inspector O'Hara reported on 16 April also (document 41), and much of what he wrote was now in response to allegations made in various media, a clear sign that the police were attempting to respond to the issues on the ground, and wider perceptions of them as reflected in newspapers.

A special meeting of Limerick corporation was held on 20 April, during which angry speeches were made over the sentencing of the boy to a month in prison. A petition for clemency was sent to the lord lieutenant. These speeches capture the intensity and emotional involvement of a number of the people in Limerick as recorded by the *Limerick Chronicle* on 21 April (document 42).

Raleigh served his sentence and was released from Mountjoy on 12 May. District Inspector O'Hara reported that it had been the intention of the boy's friends to 'have a demonstration with a band and to march round the Jewish quarter'. He had warned the band and all concerned that such a demonstration would not be allowed, and in the end, according to O'Hara, 'only a few people took part in the affair which was confined to the locality in which Rahilly lives'. There were no disturbances, he told Dublin Castle.[132]

Readers of the *Limerick Leader* got a very different account of the homecoming (document 43), in fact a complete contrast to O'Hara's report, in terms of the crowd and atmosphere, in which Raleigh's fifteen minutes of fame was wildly celebrated.

*

Other instances of assault are recalled by Fanny Goldberg in her unpublished memoirs. David Weinronk and Louis Goldberg were taking their accustomed stroll through Colooney Street when, she explains,

> father was struck on the head and fell to the ground. His shout probably saved David a similar blow. He turned quickly and got a lesser blow in the face. A big burley man

with a black shillelagh was flailing it about and shouting, 'I'll kill those bloody Jews.' Somebody picked father from the ground and he asked to be put in a side car and taken to Barrington's Hospital. This was quite a distance away. His head was bleeding profusely and I don't know how he could have got to the hospital on his own. I don't know how David Weinronk got home, but he was put to bed where he remained for some days suffering from shock. He gave mother and Bubba [grandmother] the news about father, and they were terror stricken. Father got home sometime later with stitches in his head and was in bed for a while. The shock upset him very much.

The police report of the same incident differed on some details and did not not record others (document 44).

Weinronk, according to Gerald Goldberg, suffered a broken leg and was unable to appear in court when the attacker was brought to justice (document 45).

The accused was declared insane and was sent to the local asylum. There the authorities declared that he was sane and he was released the following day. Another casualty was David Weinronk's wife, Sophia. She was, according to Fanny Goldberg, 'such a small little creature'. Venturing out one day to get some food during the troubles, she was attacked by a few young men in Bowman Street, off Colooney Street. One youth 'beat her head against the wall'. It was not clear how she managed to get away, 'but she too was in bed after that for a few weeks'. Violence was ever close during those early months of the boycott.

DOCUMENT 37
LIMERICK LEADER
ARTICLE
15 APRIL 1904

*The article reports
that the
magistrates said
they had let people
off with warnings
for similar offences
but as hostilities
were not
decreasing they
would have to 'put
down their foot'*

THE JEWISH TROUBLES

CITY PROSECUTION

BOY SENT TO JAIL

Scene in Court

At the City Petty Sessions to-day, before Mr E F Hickson, R M (presiding), and Mr S Lee, a young lad named John Rahilly, who is not quite fifteen, years, was charged with throwing a stone at and striking the Mr Levin, Chief Rabbi of the Jewish Community in Limerick. District Inspector O'Hara prosecuted, and Mr R Nash, solicitor, appeared for the defendant.

Mr Leivn in reply to Mr O'Hara, deposed that on the 4th of April, when passing by Carey's Row with two companions, he saw a crowd of boys there, who threw stones at them ; the defendant struck witness with a stone on the ankle of the right foot ; he was helped home by his companions.

Cross examined by Mr Nash—He was not attended by a doctor ; he doctored himself.

To the Bench—He had been assaulted by the same boy on St Patrick's day.

Mr Nash—Then why did you not prosecute him for the assault on St Patrick's Day ?

Witness—I did not like to go into that. But if I prosecuted for all the stone throwing I can assure you that my wages would not be sufficient to pay for summonses and solicitors.

Isaac Vinegrand gave corroborative evidence.

Cross-examined by Mr Nash—He saw the defendant before in different places. He remembered the assault by the defendant on Mr Levin on St Patrick's day.

Mr Nash—Did you report it to the police ? I did not.

Why did not you ? I cannot report every case.

Mr Nash—There is a bit of row going on, and people say that the Jews are assaulted in Limerick.

Mr Levin—And so they are.

The Chairman asked Mr Levin to sit down.

Mr Levin, who remained standing said if he thought that Mr Nash was going to scandalise the Jewish community in Limerick that he would have employed counsel. He could prove forty assault cases within a fortnight.

Mr Counihan—Behave yourself. You are making a good profit out of it.

Mr Levin—I am not.

Mr Counihan—You ought to behave yourself in court, and sit down.

Mr Nash (to witness)—How many assaults do you know of ?

Witness—I don't know—too many to remember.

Abraham Vinigrand gave corroborative evidence.

Martin Kennedy, for the defence, stated he was with Rahilly on the night in question at the Trades Exhibition, and saw him to Mrs Holmes's house, Carey's-road, where they remained until 10 o'clock ; he saw accused afterwards going into his own house ; there was no crowd at Carey's-road corner at that time.

Mrs Bridget Holmes gave corroborative evidence.

Sergeant Murray said he took Rev Mr Levin to defendant's house, where he identified John Rahilly as the boy who threw the stone at him.

This closed the evidence.

Mr Nash said the case was a very shady one, the evidence proving that the defendant was not there at the particular time mentioned. That was the evidence of two respectable witnesses. There was a lot of talk about rows or assaults on the Jews, and some London papers stated that the Jews and Jewesses were not able to walk the streets. He (Mr Nash) was walking the streets of every part of the city day and night, and he saw a great many Jews and Jewesses there, and no one to lay a wet finger on them. These statements as to the assaults were merely fabrications. In all probability these rows were being got up that money may flow into the coffers of the community in Limerick. On the evidence of the prosecution the magistrates could not convict.

Mr Levin—May I be permitted to say a few words on behalf of the Limerick Community in the city as to the very strong insinuations made by Mr

Mr Hickson—I think you had better sit down, Mr Levin.

Mr Levin—All right, your worship. Thank you.

Mr Hickson said there was no doubt from the evidence brought before the court that this boy was guilty of the assault. The attempt at an alibi made it clearer on the evidence of the other boy that he was there, and it brought him a few yards nearer to the place. He thought the evidence of the Vinegrand could not be stronger, fairer, or more moderate, and they identified the defendant as one who had given them constant annoyance by throwing stones and insulting them on the public streets on several occasions It was a very sad thing that young boys should be guilty of this. Of course they were not responsible —of course other parties were responsible for this crusade against the Jews. He did not know who these parties were, no evidence with regard to that had been produced. But these boys perpetrated the assaults and should be punished. It was well known that he (Mr Hickson) had a great objection to send young boys to jail, as there by association they got a knowledge of crime they otherwise would not obtain, but the magistrates had an unpleasant duty to perform— that was to protect every person, no matter who he was, in the city from any interference with his lawful rights. They had had a case of this kind up before the court previously, they had left them off with fines, and he had given as good advice as he could, but still the assaults were continued, and the magistrates would have to put down their foot. The defendant would have to go to jail for one month without hard labour (sensation in court).

Defendant (who was crying)—Your worships —

Defendant's mother—Oh, Lord ! Let my boy speak himself.

Mr Hickson—One month without hard labour.

Defendant's brother (from the body of the court)—I am the boy's brother. It is a very hard case to send him to jail.

Mr Hickson—Sit down.

Defendant—I was never in court before. It is my first offence. I never went near them.

Mr Nash asked to have the penalty increased to allow of an appeal. The application was reasonable having regard to the evidence, and he did not think the magistrates could legally object.

Mr Hickson—There is nothing in the case that we can give a heavier sentence—a month's imprisonment.

Defendant—I beg your pardon, I was never in the court before. I deny the charge against me.

The defendant, who cried bitterly, was then taken into custody, his mother also weeping loudly.

A NEW IRISH INDUSTRY—THE MANUFACTURE OF "INTOLERANCE."

If Limerick to-day does not bear the reputation of being the most intolerant and bigot-infested city in Ireland, it is not the fault of pious Mr SLOAN, M.P., of Belfast, or the Dublin Protestant Press. Through the medium of the latter the anti-Catholic population of the country are fed to their heart's content with plenty of savoury mental food in the shape of letters of lament and complaint at the " awful and deplorable condition," " the sad plight," " the boycotting and starvation " of the Jewish community. There is not a section in Limerick, whether it be Jewish, Catholic, or non-Catholic, that can justly accuse the LEADER of being an organ that countenances bigotry or persecution on the part of any class in our midst We make this statement not by way of an apology for, but in justification of, our attitude in regard to the Jewish question in Limerick. Therefore, when we protest in the strongest possible manner against the movement that is being set on foot to cast a slur on the fair fame of our city we do so, not in the spirit of partiality, or as Catholics, but as a duty in common justice to the public. Because of recent utterances against the methods adopted by Jewish traders in Limerick, certain persons who are bitter enemies of everything Catholic, and who have connection with institutions known by the name of " Mission to the Irish Roman Catholics," and " Irish Mission to the Jews," or some such appellation, have eagerly availed of this, to them, splendid opportunity to vilify the conduct of the Catholic population of this city. The Dublin libeller of the Very Rev Father M'Inerney, the saintly pastor of Killaloe, publishes letters day after day which set forth for the information of is reader, an extraordinary state of affairs in Limerick. A Limerick correspondent of a London evening paper not long since libelled the city by proclaiming that it was in a state of seige. Meetings of the Mission above referred to are being held in Dublin to " protest against the persecution of the Jews in Limerick ;" and we read in Lord ARDILAUN's precious organ that, " from what one hears on all sides, it does seem more than necessary that not only should the public, but especially the Irish Government, be enlightened with regard to the un-Christian and unlawful conduct manifested towards the Jews in Limerick." And further, that " such is the serious state of affairs in that city that at the annual meeting of the Society for the Promotion of Christianity among the Jews held the other day in Dublin, a very strong resolution of protest was unanimously passed against the present treatment of the Jews." And the pious Mr. SLOAN, in the House of Commons last night, asked the Chief Secretary " if his attention had been called to the refusal to deal with the intimidation of members of the Jewish persuasion, and to the fact that in some cases violence had been used, and many are at present starving by the refusal of dealers and shopkeepers to sell to them, and will he order an inquiry into the whole matter with the view of protecting the rights of these people ?" The amount of truth that is contained in all these statements may be measured by the fact that the people of Limerick are themselves in actual ignorance of those awful doings in their midst. The Chief Secretary, while he admitted that in some cases trade has been stopped with the Jews, stated that " it is not correct to say that individuals are starving." It is in this manner that reckless statements have been diffused broadcast through the country to the detriment of the good name of Limerick city. True, there were, as the Chief Secretary stated in the House last night,

said, were pending. One of these cases came before the court to-day. It was the case in which an irresponsible youth was charged with molesting the chief of the Jewish community. With his conduct, if the charge against him be true, or with that of the eight others referred to, the general body of the public have no sympathy. The acts of molestation are those of irresponsible parties, but the interested persons who write letters to the Dublin Protestant papers, proclaim to the world that all Catholic Limerick is in a ferment and in open hostility to the Jews. As a matter of fact it is those interested parties who are responsible for any hostility, if such exists, because by their libellous statements they are going the right way towards stirring up sectarian feelings. The whole Jewish question is not one of faith or belief, but one purely and simply of trade methods. This, Father Creagh made very plain in the columns of the Northern Whig, a Belfast Protestant paper, which published the whole facts of the case, as a result of their own representative's interview with Father Creagh while the latter was on a mission to that city not long since. But the Church Mission people make sure to proclaim that this is a sectarian question, and that the Jews are accordingly persecuted to an awful extent. As proof of the " intolerable " state of affairs in the city, Lord O'Brien, in opening the City Assizes last month, said to the Grand Jury—" I am glad to say that the city of Limerick is, so far as my information goes, in a satisfactory condition ;" while Judge Adams a few days since just barely missed adding another pair of white gloves to his already extraordinary collection, which, as a London contemporary wrote, " must now far exceed that of any other judge on circuit in those islands." The source of his supply is the usual peaceable condition of Limerick, yet we are asked to believe that Limerick is now in a deplorable condition. We are rather inclined to think that the Jews themselves are not free from blame in regard to the exaggerated reports that have been sent broadcast through the country. Here is what the Rabbi of the local community says in a letter which appeared in a recent number of the Jewish Chronicle :—" It is with deepest sorrow I have to inform you that the condition of my poor community is deplorable. The oppression and affliction which the Redemptorist priest, Creagh, has brought upon us, is really too heartbreaking to attempt to describe. Owing to the boycott of the Jews' trades in Limerick the majority of the thirty-five families resident here are absolutely destitute." Epistles of this and of the kind that are appearing in the Dublin Protestant press, are not calculated to peace, but to create ferment. For that reason we regret that the Jews should lend themselves to the so called Missionaries whose sole object seems to be to create a bitter feeling against Catholics. In a word these people are merely engaged in manufacturing a special species of intolerance for application to the Catholics of Limerick, which, needless to say, will be lavishly used to their " credit " wherever possible. With regard to the case in court to-day we think it rather hard treatment to the youthful defendant that he should be sent to imprisonment for one month without the option of a fine, or without the option of having a further hearing on appeal. Had the accused been a person of mature years there would be some reason in the " justice " meted out to-day, but when it is remembered that he is a young boy, irresponsible for his actions—and further, a first offender—the sentence of the Bench is nothing if not extremely harsh. We cannot help regretting, too, that there was not a single Catholic magistrate at the hearing of the case.

DOCUMENT 38
LIMERICK LEADER
EDITORIAL
15 APRIL 1904

The editorial remarked that the sentence was extremely harsh especially given that the defendant was 'a young boy, irresponsible for his actions'

APRIL 16, 1904.

Document 39 (left)
Northern Whig
Article
16 April 1904

*The editorial stated
that the sudden
backlash against the
Jews is 'partly one
of revenge for the
treatment of the
French
Redemptorists'*

JEW-BAITING IN LIMERICK.

Stoning a Rabbi.

The "Daily Telegraph" says:—As the result of a sermon preached by Father Creagh, a Limerick priest, the Jews in that city have been subjected to a boycott of considerable severity, and the attention of the Irish authorities has been called to it. A lad of fifteen, John Rahilly, was charged before Mr. Hickson, the stipendiary magistrate, yesterday, with being one of a number of boys who, on the night of the 4th inst., stoned the Rev. Elias B. Levi, rabbi of the Jewish community in Limerick, and two of his Hebrew companions. All the boys ran away except Rahilly, who was identified. The rabbi stated that within a fortnight forty assaults had been committed on Jews in Limerick. The stipendiary said that not these boys, but persons not before the court were responsible for this crusade against the Jews. The magistrates had determined to stop it. The accused would be imprisoned for a month without hard labour. An application to have the sentence increased so as to enable an appeal to be lodged was refused. Commenting on the crusade, the "Jewish Chronicle" remarks:—"If any further evidence were needed of the gross iniquity of the present boycott, it would be found in the pathetic letter of Mr. Blond, the president of the Limerick Hebrew congregation, who finds his grocery and vegetable business deliberately attacked and destroyed. Mr. Blond challenges anybody to say whom he has wronged or overcharged. But it is safe to say that no reply will be forthcoming. The spontaneity of the agitation can be gathered from the regret with which the Christian caretaker of the synagogue surrendered his post at the demand of 'other people,' while the measure of the Irish peasants' indignation against the Jewish exploiter can be gauged by the violent methods which had to be adopted to prevent him from dealing with the hated Jew. The truth is that the movement is partly one of revenge for the treatment of the French Redemptorists' (a treatment for which the French Jews are held responsible), and partly the usual despicable religious hatred. There is more at stake in this matter than the happiness of the 35 Jewish families of Limerick."

Document 40 (right)
Weekly
Northern Whig
Article
16 April 1904

*The paper
reproduced a letter
I. Julian Grande
wrote to the Times
in response to a
letter they had
printed*

BOYCOTT OF JEWS IN LIMERICK.

Mr. Julian Grande, whose letter on the above subject was published some days ago, has written the following to the "Times" in reply to a correspondent:—

Your correspondent is greatly in error in thinking that the present boycott and persecution of the unfortunate Jews in Limerick are "merely financial and not religious." Perhaps the following few extracts from Father Creagh's memorable sermon, as reported in several Irish papers, will be sufficient to enlighten even "Milesian" as to the true and incontestable cause of the sad plight of the Jews in Limerick. The following extracts are from the daily papers:—

"It would be madness for a man to nourish in his own breast a viper that might at any moment slay its benefactor with its poisonous bite. So it is madness for a people to allow an evil to grow in their midst that will eventually cause them ruin. Now, to what danger, then, did he allude to-night—what evil did he wish to direct their attention? It was that they were allowing themselves to become the slaves of Jewish usurers. They knew who those were. . . They rejected Jesus. . . They persecuted the Christians from the beginning. . . Nowadays they dare not kidnap and slay Christian children, but they will not hesitate to expose them to a longer and even more cruel martyrdom by taking the clothes off their back and the bit out of their mouth. . . Twenty years ago, and less, Jews were known only by name and evil repute in Limerick. They were sucking the blood of other nations, and they are come to our land to fasten themselves on us like leeches. . . The Jews came to Limerick apparently the most miserable tribe imaginable. . . . They have wormed themselves into every form of business. They are in the furniture trade, the mineral water trade, the milk trade, the drapery trade, and in fact into business of every description. . . Are the Jews a help to religion? I do not hesitate to say that there are no greater enemies of the Catholic Church than the Jews. If you want an example look to France. What is going on at present in that land? The little children are being deprived of their education. No nun, monk, or priest can teach in a school. The little ones are forced to go where God's name is never mentioned—to go to Godless schools. The Jews are in league with the Freemasons in France, and have succeeded in turning out of that country all the nuns and religious orders. The Redemptorist Fathers, to the number of 200, have been turned out of France, and that is what the Jews would do in our own country if they are allowed to get into power. In conclusion, he advised them to have no dealings in the manner he had described with the Jews. If they had any transactions with them they should get out of them as soon as possible, and then afterwards keep far away from them."

It was no exaggeration on the part of Mr. Michael Davitt when, commenting at the time on the rev. gentleman's sermon, he said:—"It was atrocious language like this which in May last was responsible for some of the most hideous crimes possible to perverted humanity in a Russian city." Father Creagh denounces the Jews with ecclesiastical indignation for having "wormed themselves into every form of business." But is this a crime? Is not industry, on the other hand, not only a social virtue, but the very basis of all virtues? If such be the doctrines taught by Father Creagh one ought not to be in the least surprised at the financial stagnation and utter want of social progress which, so unfortunately for its inhabitants, characterise for the most part the South of Ireland.

No, sir; the motives which prompted the Redemptorist Father are not to be found in the financial or economical aspects of the Jewish question, but, clearly and obviously to the unsophisticated and ingenuous mind, have their root, like all other so-called religious wars and persecutions, in the priest's perverted conception of religion. But as this is a subject outside the scope of my present subject, I will not make any other observation thereupon.

In conclusion, sir, allow me once more to repeat that the boycott still prevails, and the condition of the Limerick Jews is most lamentable. May I express my fervent hope that the leaders of the British Jewry will not delay in coming to the rescue of their persecuted and boycotted brethren in Limerick?

In accordance with requisition a special meeting of the Whole House Committee of the Corporation convened by the Mayor was held in the Council Chamber, Town Hall, last evening for the purpose adopting a memorial to His Excellency the Lord Lieutenant on behalf of the boy John Raleigh sentenced to one month's imprisonment at the last Petty Sessions (and since removed from Limerick prison to Mountjoy) on the charge of assaulting the Rev. E. B. Levin, Minister of the Jewish community here. The circular added that—"It is also considered desirable, to avail of the occasion to refute certain statements injurious to the character and good name of the citizens of Limerick that have recently been given to the public."

The Mayor presided. There were also present —Aldermen Prendergast, Duly, McNeice, P. McDonnell, J.P.. Councillors Johnson, King, O'Malley, C. Ryan, J. Ryan, Bradshaw, J. F. Barry, J.P.; M'Inerney, Walsh, Shanahan, Slattery, Clune, Kelly, Dalton, Murphy, Leahy, Dooley, Donnellan, M. Prendergast; Hassett, R. Nash, J. Guinane, J.P.

Mr. Killeen, Assistant Town Clerk read the requisition for the meeting which was signed by— Aldermen T. J. Prendergast, Daniel McNeice, John O'Brien, Councillors Joseph Ryan, Michael Murphy, John Slattery, Charles Johnson.

Mr. Barry proposed :—" That we the Borough Council of Limerick in Whole House Committee assembled, desire in the strongest manner to support the prayer of the memorial now got up, and we appeal to His Excellency the Lord Lieutenant to exercise his clemency and prerogative in this case, which we believe, is one, when His Excellency is made aware of the facts, we have no doubt, will be dealt with by his Excellency in a humane manner, considering the youth of the prisoner." Mr. Barry said he thought that on account of the boy's age—under fifteen—when the Lord Lieutenant was made aware of the facts of the case he would see his way to let the boy out. He (the speaker) was sure there was no member of the Council, or any citizen of Limerick; no matter what his creed or politics might be, but would denounce any violence to the Jews. He thought the resolution would have the desired effect, and also that the city would continue in the peaceable way in which it had been up to the present (hear, hear).

Mr. Johnson, in seconding the resolution, said that he knew Raleigh to be a most respectable little boy, and very unlikely to do any violence to the Jews or anyone else, and even if he did—and there was a good deal of doubt about it—he had been sufficiently punished already. In the interests of good will, which these people (the Jews) seemed so anxious to have in the city, he hoped the Lord Lieutenant would see his way to release the boy. To see the boy in convict garb would bring tears to one's eyes. His poor mother and the rest of his family were to be sympathised with.

The Mayor said that they all sympathised with the resolution, not alone the members present, but the entire body of their fellow-citizens. The punishment meted out in the case was rather severe, especially taking into account the boy's youth, and he (the Mayor) hoped that when proper representation was made, it would have the desired effect.

The resolution was passed unanimously.

THE GOOD NAME OF THE CITY.

The Mayor, proceeding, said there was far more than a personal aspect to concern them arising out of a condition of things affecting the well-being and the good name of the city of Limerick. There had been correspondence going on for some time which was highly detrimental to the interests of their city, and it was time that some one would express an opinion on the real facts of the case. It had been said that a certain community in their city were being persecuted. There was

DOCUMENT 41 (left)
O'HARA REPORT
16 APRIL 1904

O'Hara's report answered the allegations made in the press about the Limerick situation

DOCUMENT 42 (right)
LIMERICK
CHRONICLE
21 APRIL 1904

The article reproduced some of the speeches made in support of John Rahilly

continued on next two pages

no religious persecution going on in Limerick (hear, hear.) As regards the Jewish question, religion did not enter into or arise in the matter. The only objection to the Jews was their usurious methods of dealing, and the consequent hardship inflicted by them on the poor people of Limerick. There was no violence being offered to the Jews in Limerick. There was no combination against them, and the statements made in court and appearing in some sections of the Press as to assaults being committed on them, were unfounded and untrue. There was no doubt that one or two cases might arise where individuals were concerned. Such a circumstance would arise and had arisen, and would continue he supposed till the end of time in the best regulated communities. But he thought he could state without fear of contradiction that the peace, orderliness, and good conduct of the citizens of Limerick had never been surpassed in any period of its existence (hear, hear.) The official records proved that. It was a mere accident that they had not a repetition of the presentation of white gloves—so frequently made to the County Court Judge—at the last Quarter Sessions; and at the Assizes the criminal list was very small, considering the importance of the city of Limerick, its population and other causes (hear, hear). Therefore it was a very lamentable state of things—the statements that had gone abroad—and one that he referred to with very deep pain and regret. There had been at all times the most friendly and most good-natured feelings entertained by the different denominations in the city of Limerick for each other, and he would regard it as a calamity now if there was anything to come in to disturb the good feeling of friendship and brotherhood that had been so long and so well maintained between the different creeds in the the city. It was regrettable that a very high ecclesiastic should have made reference in a certain place to the condition of things existing in Limerick which it was not in his (the Mayor's) mind within the power of anyone to cavil at or find fault with. There might be under currents at work for a special purpose, and to disturb the peace of the city but he hoped the good sense of the citizens of Limerick would be sufficient to counteract any such evil influences and that they would not permit any consideration either from within or without to tarnish the good name of Limerick (hear, hear). They were well aware from time to time things were often done to serve a purpose, and made to represent a locality—aye, and the locality often times made to represent the Nation, when there was anything disparaging or derogatory to the interests of their common country. Such things were so frequent in their history that for a long time he did not take any notice of them. What he saw enacted in their midst, he thought were the usual every day occurrences in a large community, but they had now assumed a position of importance when he saw these things taken up by the English Press, and the Press generally, and published broadcast as plain truths. He said as Mayor of the city of Limerick that the peace and good conduct of the citizens were a credit to any community in the world (hear, hear). It was a feeling of great pleasure to him during his term of office to have recourse to all classes of the city, and to find that things were working so harmoniously and would continue so, he hoped. It would, therefore, be really a very serious matter for anyone, no matter how important they might be, no matter how high their dignity or station might be, to do anything or say anything against the interests of their common city (hear, hear).

Alderman O'Brien who said that he was not in at the commencement of the Mayor's observations, was about referring to the sentence on the boy Raleigh, when

The Mayor explained what had taken place, and the resolution adopted.

Mr. Barry suggested that the names of the members of the Corporation should be added to the resolution.

Mr. Guinane said the Mayor and Town Clerk could sign the Mayor and Town Clerk could sign the memorial on behalf of the Corporation, at the same time the names of the members could be affixed to it.

Mr. Johnson said he understood there was a resolution to be proposed condemning Doctor Bunbury for the attack he made on the city—for the language he used insulting to the people of the city, and their most respected Father Creagh. He did not think it should be left pass unnoticed no more than Raleigh's case. He (the Bishop) had seemingly taken his whole cue from the very truthful Chief Rabbi. The Rabbi had said a good many untruths that were noticed in the speech. For instance, it was stated that the Jews did not charge a sixpence more for their goods than the respectable traders of the city. Well he (Mr. Johnson) could prove that they charged more than 80 per cent above the dearest house in Limerick for their goods. Another portion of the speech stated that the Jews could not charge too much for tea because they never sold it. Hundreds in Limerick knew that they had sold and did sell tea. He supposed they charged 100 per cent more than the dearest house in Limerick.

Mr. King said with regard to the question of tea he had an interview that day with two ladies who used to deal with the Jews for tea and got it more than once. He did not ask them what they paid for it.

Mr. Johnson said that it showed the truthfulness of the Rabbi's evidence which condemned Raleigh.

Mr. Prendergast said that he saw tea sold by the Jews and that there was no question that they were selling the article.

Alderman McNeice said the meeting was summoned to deal with the requisition with regard to the boy Raleigh, and he did not think they should deal with anything in reference to Bishop Bunbury.

The Mayor said having regard to the memorial on behalf of Raleigh, there was no time to summon a special meeting of the Corporation, and he had called a meeting of the Whole House Committee, which was practically a Corporation meeting.

Mr. Prendergast—I think there ought to be a resolution to deal with a matter which is wrong and injurious to the citizens of Limerick. I have seen these people—the Jews—passing through the streets in different parts of the city and never saw them offended or in any way assaulted. I think a terrible lot of wrong has been done to our people and I believe done purposely to get money for the Jews.

Mr. Sheehan agreed with Mr. Prendergast. He was living in a congested portion of the city and had seen Jews going through laneways and never saw them molested.

The Mayor said statements were made by a learned ecclesiastic, in a high position, injurious to the city and their fellow-citizens, and if there was any gentleman present not satisfied with his (Mayor's) reply, it would be open to him to propose a resolution.

Alderman McNeice said he thought the Mayor had fully refuted the feeling of the city with regard to the Jews. He had stated that there was a gross misrepresentation of the facts, and he was quite sure the Council would endorse everything the Mayor had said, as would every fair minded man, no matter what his religious persuasion was.

Ald. O'Brien—We accept the Mayor's statement, and exonerate him from not being in court on Friday last.

Mr. Johnson wanted the matter to take the form of a resolution.

The Mayor—I am in your hands.

Mr. Donnellan said the chief point they had to consider was the statement put forward by a learned ecclesiastic outside the city of Limerick, relative to this Jewish question. They all regretted the use of intemperate language by any person, whether he be a high dignatory or the lowest subject of this Empire. There was one chief

subject of this Empire. [...]
point in the entire circumstances they all regretted and that was that a rev. gentleman who
made use of these remarks prejudicial to the
interests of the city should take them from a contaminated source—from those immediately concerned, the Jews themselves. He spoke in the
language of hyperbole, making use of expressions
outside or enlarging on the truth. Dr. Bunbury,
he felt sure, would be very slow to make use of
the remarks he did if they were not conveyed to
him, and they all deeply regretted that he was
led into an error. As far as the question of the
Jews in Limerick went, he (Mr. Donnellan)
was one of those who believed that their presence
in the city was not needed. It had come under
his own notice that these people charged 100 per
cent on their goods, and he was thoroughly satisfied that this was a trade and not a religious
question.

Mr. Prendergast—Nor is it.

Mr. Donnellan—It is sought to be made a
religious question, and I regret it should be so.
There is one point we should consider and that is
the usurious trading of Jews with our people,
and we as citizens of Limerick ought to and will
resent this (hear, hear). They were living in
this city in a colony by themselves, trading and
dealing amongst themselves, and we have our
own people walking the streets in thousands, and
going to America to seek a livelihood; and Jews
come in and make a living, and I hold they
should not be encouraged (hear, hear). Statements have been made as to the origin
of the subject, and a rev. gentleman we all respect
—Father Creagh—has been dragged into it. I
believe that Father Creagh's action was not
prompted by religion but merely from a commercial standpoint, and for the well-being of the
poor. I emphasise that these people should not
be permitted to trade as they are, and I hope we
have heard the last of the matter. It is to be
regretted that Bishop Bunbury was led into
error in accusing the people of Limerick of conduct
they were not guilty of.

Mr. Prendergast said when Dr. Bunbury was
raised to the Episcopal Bench the Corporation
passed a resolution congratulating him and entertained nothing but the kindliest feelings towards
him. He was then as a learned gentleman, most
pleasant to the people and so long as he did not
interfere with them he would always continue
to be esteemed, but he had now gone outside his
duty in censuring the citizens without having the
actual facts of the case.

The Mayor hoped that any money due to the
Jews would be paid to them. He had considerable experience of them in the Court of Conscience, and always treated the Jew and Gentile
alike, and would continue to do so.

Mr. Johnson then proposed, and Mr. O'Malley
seconded, the following, which was unanimously
adopted—" That we condemn and repudiate in
the most emphatic manner the attacks made by
Dr. Bunbury on the good name of our city, and
also by the English Press, and we consider such
attacks most unjustifiable and uncalled for."

THE DUKE OF NORFOLK'S ACTION.

At the request of the Jewish Board of Deputies
made through Mr. Benjamin Cohen, M.P., the
Duke of Norfolk transmitted to Cardinal Logue
the Board's letter asking for His Eminence's intervention on behalf of the Jews in Limerick. We
understand that in a note consenting to transmit
the letter the Duke spoke of having heard with
indignation and distress of "the Limerick matter,"
and added that it had given him very great
pleasure to forward the letter with an expression
of his Grace's own hope that it might receive
favourable attention.

THE JEWISH TROUBLE
RELEASE OF THE BOY RALEIGH
HIS RECEPTION IN LIMERICK
A Prison Incident

The young lad, John Raleigh, 2, Carey's-road,
who was sentenced to a month's imprisonment for
alleged stone-throwing at the Jewish Rabbi, Mr
Levin, was released from Mountjoy Prison, yesterday, and reached Limerick last evening. A large
crowd assembled at the railway station to give him
a popular welcome home, and to record their protest against the harsh sentence of a month's imprisonment without the option of a fine, and further to record their belief in his innocence of the
charge that had been brought against him.

A Presentation

On alighting from the train he was loudly
cheered, and was then taken on the shoulders of
some of his admirers and thus conveyed to his
home where he was made the recipient of a silver
watch and chain on behalf a number of friends, as
a token of their sympathy. There were present—
Messrs C Johnson, B C; M Coffey, T Looney, M
Meade, &c. The presentation was made by Mr Johnson, who expressed the sympathy the public had
for him on account of the harsh sentence he received.

A Prison Incident

To-day a LEADER representative had an interview with young Raleigh, who told him some of
his prison experiences, one incident of which deserves notice.

After the sentence at the Police Court, the youth
was removed to Limerick Jail where he was detained for six days, and then brought to Mountjoy,
Dublin, where he finished his term.

Asked had he anything to say as to his treatment, he replied that he had not, but an incident
happened in Mountjoy which shows the feeling
that has been created over the Jewish question.

" The morning after my arrival in Mountjoy,"
said Raleigh, " when I was released from my cell,
a certain warder came to me and said ' Come here
you Limerick Jew slayer.' The warder then called
three other warders and said to them—' Here is our
Limerick Jew slayer.' "

Did he give you any trouble after that? the
LEADER representative asked Raleigh.

" No, but I reported him to the chief warder," he
replied.

" It was about two hours after the incident
occurred that I got the chance," resumed the young
lad. "When I mentioned it to the chief warder, he
asked me if I could point out the man who made
use of the expression, and I said I could but I would
not, as I thought it would be worse for me during
the time I was to be in jail."

Young Raleigh, it should be mentioned, is looking well after his experience.

DOCUMENT 43
(previous page on right)
LIMERICK LEADER
13 MAY 1904

Report on Rahilly's
homecoming; the
article states that
'a large crowd
assembled … to
give him a popular
welcome home,
and to record their
protest against the
harsh sentence'

DOCUMENT 44
(this page and
opposite left)
POLICE REPORT
17 JULY 1904

Report on the
incident involving
David Weinronk
and Louis
Goldberg being
assaulted by Pat
Berkery

DOCUMENT 45
(opposite page on right)
LIMERICK LEADER
ARTICLE
22 JULY 1904

Report on the
incident involving
Weinronk, Gold-
and Berkery

Assault on Jews.

City of

Docks 17. 7. 04

I beg to state that at 1.35 or p.m today two Jews, named Louis Goldberg, No 67 Henry St, and David Weinronk, No 68 Henry St, were assaulted while walking in Colooney St, near the Military Road.
The two men named above were going home when they met Pat Berkery, of Dromkeen, who had a heavy stick in his hand, and without saying a word to either Louis Goldberg or David Weinronk. he attacked the D.I.

them with the stick and struck David Weinronk on the head, behind the left ear, and knocked him down, he also struck him with the stick on his legs while lying on the

ground. Weinronks head is swollen. but not cut. He has been attended by Doctor Fogarty who stated that he does not believe that his skull is fractured as there no bleeding from the ear.

While David Weinron was lying on the groun Pat Berkery struck

struck Louis Goldbe with the same stic on the back of the head and knocke him down. Louis Goldberg received a scalp wound; h went to Barringto Hospital and got his wound dressed and returned home Const O'Brien witness the assault, and he arrested Berkery while in the act of making a second blow at David Weinrock's head. He is detained in

---

custody here. I will take him to the Police Court tomorrow and have him re-manded. He was sober when arrested and the only remark he made was "Ye are robbing the country & I intend to do away with ye"

Berkery is a tramp labourer, unmarried, but frequently lives with his brother at Dromkeen. He stated to me that he did not feel well lately which would lead one to believe from the unprovoked assault on the Jews that his mind may be going wrong.

W Beckett. S46933

THE JEWS
ALLEGED RECENT ASSAULT
POLICE COURT PROCEEDINGS
Accused Sent to the Asylum

Patrick Berkery, a labourer from Dromkeen, was brought up in custody to-day at the City Petty Sessions charged with having, on Sunday, the 17th ult, in Colooney-street, assaulted David Weinrok and Louis Goldberg, Israelites, and in-flicted on them grievous bodily harm. Mr F M Fitt, solicitor, appeared for Mr Weinrok.

Head-Constable Webster asked the prisoner if there was any solicitor appearing for him.

Berkery—No, sir.

Mr Fitt said he appeared for Weinrok, who was so badly injured on the occasion, and that he was still confined to the house. He would produce the certificate of Dr Fogerty to that effect. He had asked Dr Fogerty when Weinrok would be able to attend, in case the magistrates put the question to him, and the reply of the doctor was, in about a fortnight. The other complainant, Louis Goldberg, was present, he understood.

Louis Goldberg was then sworn, and in answer to the Head-Constable, he deposed that on Sunday last, between one and two o'clock, he was coming from the Synagogue with Weinrock, when they met the prisoner near Mannix's, at the corner of Colooney-street; witness did not know Berkery, who struck witness first; then Mr Weinrock on the back of the head; he then struck Mr Wein-rock again, and next witness; there was no other person present that witness saw; witness had to get his wound dressed at the hospital, and had to attend daily for the purpose.

Head-Constable Webster—Did Berkery say any-thing to you before he struck you?

Witness—He said "robbers, I must do away with you." In answer to the court, Berkery said he had no questions to ask.

Head-Constable Webster said there was a deposi-tion made by Constable O'Brien, who witnessed the assault, and he would now read it for the court. The constable stated—I was on duty yesterday, the 17th inst, on the Military-road at 2 30 o'clock; I there saw the defendant, now pre-sent, Patrick Berkery; I saw him turn up Colooney-street; I saw two Jews coming down Collooney-street, and I saw him go up and strike one of them, David Weinrock, with a stick (pro-duced); he struck him on the back of the neck and knocked him down to the ground, and when on the ground struck him again with the stick, and was in the act of striking him a third time with the stick when I took it from him; he said "Let out of the stick; they are bad devils; they have persecuted the country, and I intend to do for them"; I also saw him strike Louis Goldberg another of the Jews, on the back of the head with a stick, and knock him to the ground.

That deposition was taken before the Mayor, Mr Donnelly.

Constable O'Brien stated that what was sworn in the deposition was all true.

Prisoner did not ask any questions.

Mr DeCourcey, Clerk of Petty Sessions, said there was a letter from the medical officer of the jail, Dr M'Grath, with regard to the mental condi-tion of the prisoner, and the Dispensary Medical Officer, Dr Mulcahy, was present.

Mr Guinane—Does the prisoner wish to make any statement.

Prisoner—No, sir.

Dr Mulcahy was then called and decided to make a personal examination of the prisoner. He did so, and subsequently deposed that Berkery was insane.

Mr Guinane - In that case you will have to send him to an asylum.

Mr Fitt—There is no other course open in view of the doctor's certificate.

Both cases were accordingly adjourned, and an order was made for the transmission of Berkery to

The Position of
the Church of Ireland
Bishop of Limerick

At its meeting on 20 April Limerick corporation heard strong criticism of the local Church of Ireland bishop, Dr Thomas Bunbury, who at the general synod of the Church of Ireland in Dublin on 15 April had vigorously defended the Jews of Limerick. He explained the 'persecution' of the Jews in his city to the general synod, stating that he was relying on information received from Rabbi Levin. The bishop was applauded when he related that the Jews did not charge one sixpence more on their goods than the respectable shopkeepers of Limerick.[133] He was also applauded when he said that the Jews in his city bought from wholesalers and that they made merely the legitimate profits allowed by those wholesale houses. Another accusation brought against them, he said, was that they went into country districts and, finding the parents absent, persuaded children or servants to accept goods, saying that they would call again for the money. Tea in particular was mentioned in that connection; it had been alleged that Jews left a 1lb parcel of tea at a house and then overcharged for it. Bunbury said that he had asked Rabbi Levin about this, and Levin had replied that the Jews never did anything of the sort as they did not deal in tea. The people who went about the country were a different body known as teamen. That was a complete answer to the charge, the bishop told the synod to loud applause.[134]

Bunbury then spoke of the 'persecution' of Jews in Limerick, which was 'very severe'.[135] He did not think that there had been a more severe case of boycotting. Money had been collected in London and other places for the support of the local community. He explained that the Jews were not allowed to practise their trade and that money due to them could not be recovered. They did not bring actions in the courts for the recovery of this money. They were most forbearing in their dealing, the bishop said, and they were willing to accept small instalments spread over a considerable period of time. But despite all that, they were hooted at and assaulted in the streets. When summonses were issued for such assaults and the offenders appeared in court, the magistrate did not deal properly with them.[136] The bishop said he felt fully entitled to say that the 'respectable Roman Catholic laymen in Limerick were entirely opposed to this persecution'.[137]

The general synod passed a motion drawing 'the attention of His Majesty's government and all Protestant members of parliament to the persecution of Protestants and Jews in Ireland'.[138] While the ugly situation in which the Jews of Limerick found themselves might be described as 'persecution', there was no evidence that Protestants shared the same fate. Not surprisingly Bunbury's speech and the synod resolution were received very negatively in Limerick. District Inspector O'Hara explained to his superiors that the bishop had 'given offence locally as it is considered that he interfered gratuitously in a matter not concerning him and that he relied on statements made to him by the rabbi without investigating their accuracy'.[139] Members of Limerick corporation and the local press were outraged. Alderman Donnellan told the corporation meeting on 20 April that he regretted the use of 'intemperate language' by the 'learned ecclesiastic' outside the city of Limerick; the bishop had taken his information 'from a contaminated source – from those immediately concerned, the Jews themselves'.[140] As far as the question of the Jews in Limerick went, Donnellan 'was one of those who believed that their presence in the city was not needed' as 'these people' discharged 100 per cent profit on their goods.[141] The *Munster News*' editorial on 20 April vented local anger and emotion and pulled no punches in criticising the bishop's intervention (document 46).[142]

William J. Moloney, writing in the nationalist weekly, the *Leader*, felt that Rabbi Levin and his supporters exaggerated the entire episode:

> You would naturally conclude from the reading of all the rancorous flummery that has appeared in bigoted Protestant journals, that Jews in Limerick are being roasted at stakes and crucified at corners, and that those who are happy enough to escape Catholic ferocity, are hid away in their wretched hovels, starving and singing the lamentations of Jeremiah.[143]

Moloney wrote that it was 'the opinion of shrewd people in Limerick that the whole outcry is a moneymaking scheme on the part of the Jews'.[144] Bunbury, he contended, had been contradicted in every single assertion he made:

> His speech has certainly been a disgrace to his position as a high Protestant dignitary, and would have been a disgrace also to his intelligence and good taste, if he were the

happy possessor of either … It is a high tribute to the extreme moderation of the people of Limerick that they have borne almost good-humouredly, the impertinent censure of a Protestant bishop.[145]

Moloney asked whether 'we in Limerick' had to 'close our eyes to the evil influence on morality of the low-type Jews' who had come to the city during the previous twenty years: 'Ireland is, at present, being drained of its Gaelic population by emigration, and Jewish colonists are trooping in to fill up the places of the emigrants, and to turn Ireland into a filthy Ghetto.'[146]

continued on next page

The Munster News

AND

LIMERICK AND CLARE

ADVOCATE

BE JUST AND FEAR NOT.

WEDNESDAY EVENING, APRIL 20.

DR BUNBURY'S SPEECH.

WE published in our issue of Monday Bishop Bunbury's speech on the persecution of the Jews in the city, and we made some general comments on it. We now go into it a little more minutely. It was a brilliant effort. From the assurance with which he spoke before the Dublin Synod one would think that he was intimately acquainted with every lane in Limerick. Only imagine him, after a day's apostolic toil resting his weary body and worried mind, groaning like Jeremiah over the moral desolation of this city, and praying God in the evening to heal the evils he had seen during the day—and we have a picture for gods and men. To put it as plain as the nose in his face we go bail that Bishop Bunbury does not know Carey's Road from Garvey's Range, or Naughton's Lane from The Long Can.

Come now, Bishop, let us do a little light thinking together. It will have a refreshing effect on yourself, and on the public who will be our audience. Your audience at the Dublin Synod were no doubt edified and consoled by the apostolic care which gained the information you gave them.

1st—You say that you "spoke from information received from the head of the Jewish community in Limerick." That is, you made a Jew witness in his own case, swallowed the answers he gave, and found them like honey in your mouth. But can't you see that your information thus got is all on one side, like the handle of a can? You say that you "put before him the accusations brought against the Jews, and asked him to explain them," and that he explained to your satisfaction. No wonder. The shrewd Jew had as light a task in convincing such an inquirer as you, as a fellow would have in pressing a toper into a "pub" for a pint.

2nd—But, let us see how closely you cross-examined him. You asked "if they charged immense profits on their goods," but he said that "they did not charge sixpence more than the respectable shop keepers of Limerick." Now, we who have not your apostolic simplicity, would have said to him, "go, tell that to the marines." But you pressed the question, and asked if "they did not sell tea at 3s 6d a lb?" He replied that they could not, for it was not they who sold the tea at all, but somebody else. And because they don't deal in tea at 3s 6d a lb, or in tea at all, you triumphantly conclude that, therefore, they charge only the prices of "respectable shopkeepers in Limerick" for skirts, shawls, pictures, beds, boots, tables, and trumperies of all sorts. And you add, evidently satisfied with your peculiar acuteness, and your conscientious cross-examination—"That's a complete answer to the charge."

3rd—You showed up two years ago, at a Synod in Tralee, as a political economist. At the Dublin Synod you distinguish yourself in arithmetic. This is how—"The Jews are most forbearing in their dealings they willingly accept small instalments spread over a considerable time." That is to say, if a Jew sells a pair of boots, which might be bought elsewhere for 7s 6d, at the rate of 1s 0d a week for half a year, the happy purchaser would have paid only 7s 6d, besides a trifle of interest, for his boots by the time he had squared accounts with the Jew.

4th. But you are a historian, too. It is only local and recent history; but still history. You told your Dublin audience that "The Jews did not bring actions for the recovery of their money." Now, everyone who remembers the cases of that sort which have come before the Mayor's Court or Judge Adams for the last dozen years, will merely laugh at you for chewing that chestnut before your Dublin Synod. That "story" earmarks your knowledge of Limerick, and your credit in the whole affair.

5th. But you are above and before all things an apostle—and quite right. You lectured before your Dublin Synod, the Magistrates of Limerick on their duties, for you said that when cases came before them "they did not deal properly with the offenders." You lectured Father Creagh's superiors on their neglect of duty, for in pious wrath you ask, in the presence of your Dublin Synod "Why his superiors should allow him to go on in this way." You lecture the Government: for you express is treating the matter." You could teach them, all and each, their duty, and show them how to do it. You are a wonderful man!

Now, we cannot help asking—Have the Protestant bishops, parsons, and laymen nothing else to do at their Synod? If they have not, we would make a suggestion. Instead of listening to such nonsense as we have just exposed, or discussing missionaries who have come here to convert the Jews of Limerick, they would find a wide field, with their work cut out for them, if they turned their apostolic zeal to the pagan barbarians who fester in the mining districts in England, or in the slums of London. Even Moslem missionaries are lately gaining converts over to Mahommed in that Mecca of Protestantism, whilst a whole Synod in Dublin are spending time listening to and applauding a bishop talking trash about Jewish "respectable dealing" in Limerick. But those Protestant apostles will try to convert anyone except themselves, though indeed a good many of them nearer home than London could bear a lot of converting, if they did not take themselves already for "saved"? However, as they want to convert the Jews of Limerick, we would advise them to consult the heads of wholesale houses in Limerick, and they will learn which of the Commandments they should preach to the Jews. Let Dr. Bunbury, who knows everything about Limerick, ask any of those firms why they will not give the Jews a shilling credit, and he will know a little more than everything. And in their part, we would advise the Jews to take all the cash they can get from those missionaries, and from their new-born Protestant sympathisers. But let them be sure that Dr Bunbury will subscribe as much in cash as in talk. Let them look out for that, and they have our blessing. It will go worse.

Now, the Catholics of Limerick have never been aggressive towards Bishop Bunbury. The Corporation tendered their congratulation to him when he became Bishop, but he returned their politeness by making his Synod in Tralee a platform to insult them; and he went whining to St Mary's Cathedral a few weeks later, because he was answered back. He has, however, kept quiet for two years; but he revives his offensiveness in Dublin. But, let him make up his mind about it, he shall not strike without being struck back. If his Synod in Dublin or Tralee have nothing better to do, we do not object to his amusing his hearers about our conduct, provided he tells the truth. But a dozen years is a short span; and we do not forget the man who swore before Commissioners in the courthouse at one time that Leamy's School could contain 400 pupils, and at another that there was room only for 100.

Let Bishop Bunbury then behave himself, as becomes one of his social position, and he may count on the courtesy which the Catholics of Limerick have always shown him. But to bear his Synodal slander in silence would not be courtesy but cowardice; and the days are gone when a Papist, ridden over by a Protestant fox-hunter, should crawl, hat in hand, to beg his honour's pardon for having been in the horses' way. We are now in the dawn of the 20th century, but Dr Bunbury does not seem to have yet taken the cobwebs from his eyes. So wake up, Bishop, and realise that a new light has come over Ireland, that the "old order changes giving place to new, and God fulfils himself in many ways." We don't object to you trying to convert us, but we protest against your plan; we take to truths but we take no notice of nonsense.

121

The Legacy of Anti-Semitism

However, Moloney's interpretation of what was happening in Limerick did not accord with the reality of Jewish life. M. J. Blond, who was forced to sell out his trading stock, had written to the *Times* on 10 April:

> It took me all these years, with the greatest pain and trouble and working unceasingly until I established myself comfortably and enjoyed a nice trade, until, all of a sudden, like a thunderstorm, spoke hatred and animosity against the Jews, how they crucified Lord Jesus, how they martyred St Simon, and gradually in one month's time, I have none of my previous customers coming into my shop. In fact, my business is nil at present. Would you call my trade a national evil? I defy anyone in this city to say whom I have wronged, what did I overcharge ... since the beginning of the crusade of Father Creagh against the Jews we never got a fair chance to defend ourselves or to put our case rightly before the Public.[147]

Members of the Jewish community in the city, facing as they were financial ruin, offered to show their accounts in order to prove they were honest traders.[148]

Fanny Goldberg, in her memoirs, recalled that Jewish men and travellers were at a complete standstill as a consequence of the boycott. She remembered a visit to Limerick by the Jewish Board of Deputies to hold an enquiry and to raise funds for the relief of those suffering discrimination:

> I remember huge sheets of rolled foolscap came to father by post. I suppose from London. Everyone who had suffer-

ed losses (and who hadn't) came to our house and made a solemn declaration to father and to Mr [Solomon] Ginsberg who were in charge of the matter for our community. Every declaration was written out by Alec Ginsberg, the eldest son of the Ginsberg family. I do not know how much each person got in compensation, but after that came the exodus. Everybody had been ruined.

As the boycott continued into the autumn, there was a further attempt by an anonymous apologist for Creagh to fan the flames of anti-Semitism. A letter, signed by 'Lugaid', was published in the *Limerick Echo* on 1 October 1904 (document 47).

The local RIC and Dublin Castle viewed the letter as an attempt to 'kindle agitation against the Jews which had almost died out'.[149] 'Lugaid' did not get his way.

What impact did the boycott have on Jewish families in the city? This was a source of disagreement between the police authorities and the Jewish community. The county inspector, Thomas Hayes, reported on 12 March 1905 that 'the trade of the Jews has unquestionably fallen off in the city' but the Jews who trade the country 'districts' were doing 'fairly well'.[150] Another report, dated 13 March 1905, stated: 'Their trade in the city is ruined: in the country except close to Limerick City, it has fallen off.' It was also stated that 'As a general rule they are left severely alone though there are one or two exceptions.'[151]

The official estimate in March 1905 of the effect of the boycott on the population of Limerick Jews was as follows:

The police now report that, within the past year, 8 Jewish

*'Lugaid' referred
to Fr Creagh's
sermon as
'eloquent appeals'
and continued by
saying that 'our
brave priest spoke
the naked truth'*

THE JEWS IN LIMERICK.

TO THE EDITOR OF LIMERICK WEEKLY ECHO.

DEAR SIR—It is a marked and discreditable characteristic of Limerick people to inaugurate a new departure with great effusion, and leave it thenceforward without notice or support. Witness within a couple of years such noticeable instances as the Town Tenants' League, the Griffin Centenary Memorial, and latest of all, the agitation against the Jews. Six months since, when the eloquent appeals of Very Rev Father Creagh, C.SS.R, had aroused the people to a sense of imminent danger, an outsider might have hastily concluded that Limerick would be no longer a happy hunting-ground for Jews. The excitement had reached a feverish height, the local press lent their columns week by week to maintain public interest in the matter, which had attained journalistic attention in Dublin and across the water, and the impending exodus of the Jews was a favourable topic of conversation everywhere in the city. Look now on the other side of the picture—that which presents itself to-day. I need not ask if the expectations of six months ago have been in any degree fulfilled. Such a question would affront the intelligence of any one of your readers. The simple facts are that the chosen people still issue from the ghetto with clockwork regularity on Mondays to pursue their beneficent avocations throughout the week in peace, their country customers are still faithful to them, their commercial correspondents in Leeds, Manchester, etc, are still made happy by the receipt of large orders from Limerick, and the wretched creatures in the purlieus of Limerick who flouted their Jewish creditors six months ago under the pressure of public opinion, have returned like the dog to its vomit, and are again robbing their families, damning their souls and forfeiting for ever their self respect by dealing with the garbage of Europe. To what inherent defect in our character may this disgraceful *volte face* be attributed? Is it not to that peculiar suppleness of conscience which permits to say one thing whilst doing the contrary, and still be free from remorse or the self-reproach of conscious hypocrisy? When Father Creagh was boldly exposing the villanies of the Jews his denunciations found thousands of echoes inside and outside of the Arch-Confraternity, and were so generally approved of amongst the working class customers of the Jews, that he might have regarded the question as decided in his favour by the very people who had till then been the chief financial support of the Limerick Jews. Yet the Jews live otherwise in Limerick, though no manna falls from Heaven or elsewhere. I take no account here of the shameful boycott to which Father Creagh was subjected by the great majority of those shepherds of the people who should have most warmly supported him, but who remained discreetly silent whilst one brave priest spoke the naked truth and "faced the music" alone. There may have been in their cases wheels within wheels of which I am ignorant, and which may explain, though they cannot justify, an ignominious silence. Neither do I refer the failure of the movement to the aloofness of the metropolitan Catholic Press which acted up to its reptile traditions by sitting on the fence. It should have sufficed for the success of the agitation if the workingmen of Limerick had known their own minds and respected their own consciences. They ought not require outside help in dealing with a domestic question such as this, and I am convinced that if even now a determined and systematic effort were made, the Jewish colony in Limerick would be reduced to one-tenth, and would no longer be a menace to the community? Will such an effort be made? Will the manhood of Limerick, such as it is, arise and resolve, not in word but in deed, to rally round the good priest and patriotic citizen who has pointed out the evil and to organise an effective crusade against it? As the best means of bringing the matter to a head, I would suggest that a public meeting be convened by the Mayor, the President of the Catholic Literary Institute, or the President of the Trades, and that a committee be formed at such a gathering to take the matter energetically in hands. I have heard several promising plans for dealing with the problem which might then be usefully ventilated. But, if nothing be done, the result is quite clear. The humbler classes in this city are doomed for ages to come to be as Father Creagh expressed it, "the slaves of Jewish usurers." With apologies for intrusion.—I am, dear sir,
        Yours sincerely,   LUGAID.

families (49 persons) have left Limerick. Of these, 5 families left directly owing to the agitation, as the bread-winners could no longer obtain employment as 'travellers'. The other 3 families left the town for private reasons – two having arranged before 1st January, 1904, to go to South Africa, and the third because its head (a Rabbi) was no longer needed as Minister. The 5 families which left owing to the agitation number 32 persons. 26 families remain, of whom 8 only are in good circumstances.[152]

In some circles the matter was far from over. I Julian Grande, who had been active in promoting the cause of the Limerick Jews throughout 1904, was equally active in 1905. In May 1905 he forwarded Sir Otto Jaffe, the former Lord Mayor of Belfast, a draft of a letter which, he claimed, was only pulled from publication at the request of the Limerick Jews (documents 48 and 49).

The new chief secretary for Ireland, Walter Long, answered a question on the Limerick boycott in the House of Commons on 4 July 1905, using the above figures.[153] Having read the reports of the Commons debate in the press, Rabbi Levin wrote to Long on 11 July stating that, according to their community records, 'the members of the Jewish Congregation who [have] been compelled to leave Limerick owing to the boycott, violence and constant abuse brought upon us by Fr Creagh [number] 75 individuals instead of 32'.[154] It is difficult to resolve the contradiction between the conflicting figures. Whatever the number, the Jewish community in Limerick had been dealt a severe blow which threatened its viability. The Ginsbergs left. The Jaffes left. The Weinronks followed the Greenfields to South Africa. The Goldbergs left for Leeds, before Louis brought his family back to

Cork. Virtually the entire Jewish community in the city joined the exodus. The Limerick boycott was, as Louis Hyman described it, a 'sad but uncharacteristic and atypical episode' in Irish history.[155]

Life was never the same again for Rabbi Levin and the Limerick Jews.[156] Remaining in the city until 1911, the rabbi then went to Leeds, where he ministered until his death in 1936.

DOCUMENT 48
5 MAY 1905

I. Julian Grande's letter to Sir Otto Jaffe asking him to use his 'powerful influence with the Irish government'

5th May 1905.

Dear Sir Otto Jafe,

As Promised, I have much pleasure in sending you herewith a copy of the letter which I sent to the "Times"; and which the Editor, as you saw by his letter to me, was willing to publish.

But, at the special request of the Jews in Limerick, I had to telegraph to the "Times" and six other papers, asking them to postpone publication for the present.   If you can use your powerful influence with the Irish Government, it would be a great matter.   Unless the Irish Government do something, I shall be obliged to let the letter appear in the press.

Yours faithfully,

I. Julian Grande

DOCUMENT 49
(following two pages)
MAY 1906

I. Julian Grande's letter to the Times

Sir Otto Jafe J.P.,

Belfast.

To the Editor,
         of the "Times",

Sir,
         It is with deep regret that I have once again to trouble you on the
unfortunate subject of the boycott of the Jews in Limerick.   It is now
over a year since I brought before the public this matter, and, notwith-
standing, the just indignation of the enlightened people in England and
Ireland, things have not improved, but on the contrary the condition
of the remaining Hebrews in Limerick is worse than ever.   They are now no
longer stoned, but are starved.   Last year, after the protest of the
entire press and several public men, including the Duke of Norfolk, it was
hoped by all parties that those responsible for the persecution would let
matters die.   Consequently, those interested in the Hebrew community
avoided publicity, while, at the same time, they have tried to start in
life again the ruined Jews.   Their persecutor, however, who is a Roman
Catholic Priest of the Redemptorist Order, and who, as the Jews allege, is
the cause of their present trouble, made up his mind to expel every Jew
from Limerick.   He advised the people to boycott them, but not to do them
bodily harm.   After the Anti-Semitic sermon which appeared in the Nationalist press in Limerick, I called to see this Priest (Rev. Mr. Creagh),
and, after an hour's talk with him, in the course of which we discussed
fully and freely the subject,   I wrote in the "Times" (April 1st 1904) that
"I am convinced that if Father Creagh remains in the city directing its
Roman Catholicism the Jews will have to leave".   Now it is over a year
since I wrote this, and the result is that eight Jewish families comprising
fortynine persons, besides several single men, were obliged to leave Limerick
directly owing to the boycott and persecution.   Their entire trade in the
city is ruined, and one does not really know what is to become of them.
In point of fact, the condition of the remaining twentyfive Jewish families
who have held out up to the present is very much worse than last year.
The boycott has not been relaxed, but has been permanently established by
the Rev. Mr. Creagh, who has opened a shop in connection with the Arch-
Confraternity of the Holy Family to carry on business on the system
of weekly payments of small instalments.   Mr. Creagh adopted the very system for
which he ordered the people to boycott the Jews.   The only difference in
the methods is, that while the Jews sold goods on credit without security,
the goods are sold by this Church shop at ordinary retail prices on security.   The business of the Jews has been reduced by 75%.   One man who was
the principal victim of the persecution and boycott, and who had several
times been refused a decree by the Co.Court Judge for money which was due
to him, has lately died heart-broken, I have no doubt owing to the terrible
persecution to which he was subjected.   He was the honoured president of
the Jewish community in Limerick for three years.   He was a grocer and for
eighteen years he managed to support his wife and family comfortably, but
owing to the boycott he was obliged to sell his business for the petty sum
of £5.   A year ago an attempt was made to wreck his shop, and the police
who at the time were guarding the Jewish quarter day and night arrested two
men, but the police did not, for some reason or other, preferred a charge
of drunkenness and disorderly conduct against the two men, for which they
were afterwards fined 2/6 each.   I may mention here that after the two
men were arrested the police requested the Jew not to prosecute, and above
all not to make it known that there had been any attempt to wreck his shop.
I wonder by whose instructions they acted in this manner.   The same thing,
by the way, happened when a Jew was seriously assaulted in the public street.
The police in this case also advised the Jew not to prosecute, but to accept
a sum of money from the assailant who was a Roman Catholic.   Perhaps these
are matters for Mr. Long, our new Chief Secretary, to enquire into.   Of
course, there are other matters which it would be interesting for the public
to know, but this would necessitate a sworn enquiry.   The immediate matter,
however, that I wish to bring before the notice of the leading Jews in
London, and especially the Jewish Board of Deputies, is, what action they

ntend taking. The matter now admits of no delay; there is a limit of
uffering even for a Jew. Seventeen out of twentyfive families still in
imerick are wholly without resources, and literally unable to endure the
oycott any longer. They need not expect any help from the Church of
ome unless they enter Father Creagh's fold. Father Creagh is as determined
s he was when on the 11th and 12th of January 1904 he preached his
emorable Anti-Semitic sermons, and told his congregation to boycott the
ews. In case your readers have forgotten the "Christian" sermon I will
ive here an extract as it appeared in several Irish Nationalist newspapers,
n the course of which Rev. Mr. Creagh is reported to have said:-

"It would be madness for a man to nourish in his own breast a
"viper that might at any moment slay its benefactor with its poisonous
"bite. So it is madness for a people to allow an evil to grow in their
"midst that would eventually cause them ruin. Now to what danger then
"did he allude tonight--what evil did he wish to direct their attention?
"It was that they were allowing themselves to become the slaves of
"Jewish usurers. They knew who those were....They rejected Jesus....
"They persecuted the Christians from the beginning....Now-a-days they
"dare not kidnap and slay Christian children, but they will not hesitate
"to expose them to a longer and even more cruel martyrdom by taking the
"clothes off their back and the bit out of their mouth....Twenty years'
"ago and less Jews were known only by name and evil repute in Limerick.
"They were sucking the blood of other nations, and they are come to our
"land to fasten themselves on us like leeches....The Jews came to
"Limerick apparently the most miserable tribe imaginable....They have
"wormed themselves into every form of business....They are in the furni-
"ture trade, the mineral water trade, the milk trade, the drapery trade,
"and, in fact, into business of every description....Are the Jews a
"help to religion? I do not hesitate to say that there are no greater
"enemies of the Catholic Church than the Jews. If you want an example
"look to France. What is going on at present in that land? The little
"children are being deprived of their education. No nun, monk, or
"priest can teach in a school. The little ones are forced to go where
"God's name is never mentioned--to go to Godless schools. The Jews
"are in league with the Freemasons in France, and have succeeded in
"turning out of that country all the nuns and religious orders. The
"Redemptorist Fathers, to the number of two hundred, have been turned
"out of France, and that is what the Jews would do in our own country
"if they are allowed to get into power. In conclusion he advised
"them to have no dealings in the manner he had described with the Jews.
"If they had any transactions with them they should get out of them
"as soon as possible, and then afterwards keep far away from them".

May I ask those responsible for the preservation of law and order
n Ireland, is there one law for the priest and another for the layman?
s the law of conspiracy dead? Are the priests above the law? Have the
ews no right to protection, many of them loyal subjects of the King?
f the answers are in the affirmative, then I appeal to the Jews in London
o assist their poor unfortunate remaining brethren and their families to
eave Limerick, and let that lawless city get the reward from Him who has
ighteously judged Spain in the past, and is judging another semi-christian
ountry at present for their cruel treatment of God's ancient people.

Yours etc.

I. Julian Grande,
Director of the Irish Mission to the Jews

13 Upper Sackville Street,
Dublin.

25 1905

The Departure of Fr Creagh: April 1906

F r John Creagh, meanwhile, opened a bank, a shop and the Workmen's Industrial Association in autumn 1904 in order to supply the 'poorer classes with clothing etc. on the instalment payment system'. The goods were supplied at ordinary retail prices provided security was given for the weekly payments.[157] During the following two years he directed his attacks towards the abuse of alcohol, evil literature and obscenity in the theatre. In November 1905, Creagh supported Bishop O'Dwyer's condemnation of the play *Sapho* by Mrs Bandmann-Palmer which was playing at the Theatre Royal. He was in excellent form when he addressed the arch-confraternity:

> And when such a play that was against morality was pro-
> duced at the theatre he advised no one to look upon such
> foul representations because their eyes stimulated the
> mind and the imagination, and imagination easily worked
> upon the lower passions.[158]

Then, having served one term as director of the arch-confraternity, Creagh was assigned to the Redemptorist order's new missions in the Philippines in early 1906. That was in no sense a demotion. The local press paid homage to his achievements. The *Limerick Echo*, in an editorial on 24 April, spoke warmly of his successful battle:

with the usurers who grew fat on the people's want of thrift
... The blows delivered were with no uncertain aim. Nor
was the matter ended, as is only too often the case, when
the talking was done.[159]

Another press report praised the man who had founded
the Workmen Industrial Association:

To him is due the great movement dealing a great blow to
the Jews, who had begun by their methods of usury to
make life nearly intolerable for some of those poor strug-
gling people who were so foolish as to buy their articles at
most exorbitant instalment prices.[160]

The *Limerick Leader* added its voice to the chorus of
appreciation on 27 April:

To Fr Creagh is due practically the entire abolition of a
system of credit trading with hawkers which had a de-
moralising effect on the poor families owing to the exac-
tion in the shape of high interest levied for a deposit of the
commonest class of good.[161]

An editorial in the *Munster News* on 9 May also recalled
Creagh's 'success' of 1904:

Later on Father Creagh discovered that much of the
money earned by the poor people of the city was being
handed over week by week to astute Hebrew harpies who,
at that time, swarmed over the entire country and city ...
Father Creagh ... resolved to change all that; and change
it he did beyond question, and that in a very short time ...
[by removing] the blighting influence of the Jewish pedlar
from the homes of the people.[162]

The paper wondered whether his work would endure or whether he would watch from afar as the men for whom he had laboured so unselfishly 'handed themselves over to the tender mercies of the publican, the money-lender, the Jewman, the bagman, and the usurious purveyor of miscellaneous foreign shoddy'. There was no fear of that happening, the paper felt.[163]

At his final meeting of the arch-confraternity, Creagh was presented with an address which recorded his 'arduous and heroic service for the spiritual and temporal welfare' of the society. The address recalled:

> The indomitable effort you made to rescue the working classes of Limerick from the usurious grasp of foreigners planted in our midst and which resulted in a great victory, cannot easily be forgotten, and is a circumstances which will be proudly related to your credit in days yet to come by parents to their children. Let us hope that the lesson will not be forgotten when you are no longer amongst us.[164]

Fr Creagh, in his reply, stated that the establishment of the Workmen's Industrial Association had been the means of keeping the poor 'independent of the Jewish usurers'.[165] After benediction, a 'pathetic scene' took place in the church as large numbers of men crowded around the altar to shake Creagh's hand as he passed from the pulpit. At Fr Creagh's special request, the members sang the rallying song of the confraternity – 'Confraternity men to the fight'.[166]

On 12 May 1906, Creagh was seen off by a large crowd at Limerick railway station. He never returned to the city of his birth, dying in Wellington, New Zealand, in 1947.[167]

Nearly seventy years later, the Limerick county manager, Richard Haslam, discovered that the Jewish burial ground on the Dublin Road near Castleconnell had fallen into neglect. The cemetery had become overgrown and was in need of attention. Although strictly speaking the grounds were not under his jurisdiction, Haslam undertook to have the grass cut at regular intervals and an identification sign erected. He corresponded with Gerald Goldberg in Cork about the long-term upkeep of the grounds. Eventually it was decided to place the cemetery under the trusteeship of two members of the local Jewish community, the late Louis Fine and Stuart Clein.[168] Under Haslam's direction, a sum of £1,000 was voted by Limerick County Council to the Limerick Civic Trust to help restore the burial ground and pay for its upkeep.[169] The director of the trust, Denis Leonard, explained that his organisation has an indirect but ongoing role in the maintenance.[170]

An ecumenical service was held on 14 November 1990 to mark the completion of the restoration of the burial ground and prayer house.[171] The ceremony was presided over by Chief Rabbi Ephraim Mirvis, and the Catholic bishop of Limerick, Jeremiah Newman, and the Church of Ireland bishop of Limerick and Killaloe, Edward Darling, also took part. The two bishops were among those who planted six trees to mark the occasion which the Limerick Leader described in an editorial as 'possibly the most ecumenical occasion ever witnessed in Limerick'.[172] It added that the monument inaugurated that day was 'an essential part of our shared heritage, Gentile and Jew. Let us treasure it'.[173] Chief Rabbi Mirvis referred in his address to the economic boycott and attacks on the Jews in 1904: 'This is a significant but sad occasion, for while we recall a period of bitterness and suffering endured by Jewish inhabitants of the city a few generations ago, we gather today in a wonderful spirit of fraternity, harmony and peace.'[174]

That small act of official generosity, initiated by Richard Haslam and executed by the Limerick Civic Trust, meant much to Gerald Goldberg and other members of the Irish Jewish community whose families had lived through the boycott of 1904. The ecumenical ceremony was a cross-community statement that explicitly acknowledged both the historical presence of Jews in the city and county, and that Jews were – and are – an integral part of that community, a fact that the late Jim Kemmy had repeatedly chronicled in the pages of the *Limerick Journal*.

Notes

1 Dermot Keogh, *Jews in Twentieth Century Ireland: Refugees, Anti-Semitism and the Holocaust* (Cork: Cork University Press, 1998).

2 *Ibid.*

3 See Thomas Morrissey, SJ, *Bishop Edward Thomas O'Dwyer of Limerick, 1842–1917* (Dublin: Four Courts, 2003), see pp. 319–26.

4 In the course of researching *Jews in Twentieth Century Ireland* this was pointed out to Dermot Keogh by the late Gerald Goldberg whose family lived there in 1904 and were obliged to leave the city as a consequence of the disturbances.

5 P. L. S. Quinn, 'The Re-entry of the Jew into England and Ireland and His Reestablishment There' (PhD, University College Cork, 1966).

6 Louis Hyman, *The Jews of Ireland: From Earliest Times to the Year 1910* (Shannon: Irish University Press, 1972), p. 114. Up to 1880 there were never more than 350 Jews in Dublin: among them were craftsmen – gold and silversmiths, brassworkers, picture-frame carvers, watchmakers, jewellers and grocers. See Quinn, 'The Re-entry of the Jew into England and Ireland', p. 576.

7 Bernard Shillman, *A Short History of the Jews in Ireland* (Dublin: Eason, 1945), p. 134.

8 Census of Ireland, 1891 (Dr Caroline Windrum, Institute of Irish Studies, Queen's University Belfast, provided this information for Professor Dermot Keogh).

9 Hyman, *The Jews of Ireland*, pp. 208–9.

10 Gerald Goldberg, 'Note on the Jewish Community in Cork', in Shillman, *A Short History of the Jews*, p. 141.

11 *Ibid.*

12 John Crowley, 'Narrative and Place: A Cultural History of the South Parish' (MA, University College Cork, 1993), p. 80.

13 Interview with Gerald Goldberg, Cork, December 1995. Fully intending to emigrate to the United States, Louis Goldberg set out with his family on two occasions to take the boat at Cobh. He changed his mind the first time and returned to the city. The next time his daughter required medical attention after she got her hand caught in a door at the station. This he took as an omen to remain in Cork. He did so, and Cork was the richer for that decision. He died on 22 December 1932.

14 See Dermot Keogh, *Jews in Twentieth Century Ireland*, p. 8ff.

15 Michael Davitt, *Within the Pale: The True Story of Anti-Semitic Persecutions in Russia* (London: Hurst and Blackett, 1903), pp. 26–9.

16 *Ibid.*, p. 29.

17 David Cesarani, *The Jewish Chronicle and Anglo-Jewry 1841–1991* (Cambridge: Cambridge University Press, 1994), p. 70; see also Nancy and Stuart Schoenburg, *Lithuanian Jewish Communities* (New York: Garland Publishing, 1991), p. 32.

18 This is Akmian in Yiddish and its current name is Akmene. Details gleaned from letter from Len Yodaiken, Kibbutz Kfar Hanasai, to Hubert Wine, 19 February 1993. Copy of letter in manuscript of Nurock and Abrahamson family history in possession of Maurice Abrahamson, Dublin.

19 *Ibid.*

20 *Ibid.*; see also Schoenburg, *Lithuanian Jewish Communities*, pp. 401–17.

21 Shillman, *A Short History of the Jews*, p. 136.

22 Interviews with Gerald Goldberg, Cork, 1995–97.

23 This account is based on Des Ryan, 'Jewish Immigrants in Limerick – A Divided Community', in David Lee (ed.), *Limerick Remembered* (Limerick: Limerick Civic Trust, 1997), pp. 167–70.

24 With accommodation for 300 male worshippers in the body and over 150 women in the gallery, this fine edifice had been built for a total cost of £5,000. An adjoining area contained a number of schoolrooms which could hold up to 200 students.

25 Quoted in Ira B. Nadel, *Joyce and the Jews: Culture and Texts* (Gainesville: University Press of Florida, 1996), p. 186.

26 Hyman, *The Jews of Ireland*, p. 210. No satisfactory explanation has been provided for this outbreak of violence. Hyman speculates that a maid-servant in the household observed the ritual slaughter of a fowl, and anti-Jewish rumours spread in the community.

27 *Ibid.*, p. 211 (*Cork Examiner*, 25 April 1884, quoted in *Jewish Chronicle*).

28 Hyman, *The Jews of Ireland*, p. 211.

29 *Ibid.*, pp. 218–20.

30 *Ibid.*, p. 221.

31 *Ibid.*, p. 222; Another member of the Irish Parliamentary Party, Justin McCarthy, wrote on 9 May that the reports of attacks on the homes of Jews in Cork had filled him with surprise and regret:

'The Irish people are in strong political sympathy with the Jews.' He referred to Thomas Moore's frequent comparison between the Irish race and that of the 'Sad One of Zion'. McCarthy stated that the ill-treatment of Jews 'is regarded with utter detestation by every Irish nationalist'.

32 Hyman, pp. 161–2.
33 Adler to Walsh, 25 October 1886, Jewish Information Folder, Archbishop William Walsh Papers, Dublin Archdiocesan Archives (DAA).
34 Adler to Walsh, 4 November 1886.
35 'Ireland and the Jews', letter to the editor from Michael Davitt, Freeman's Journal, 13 July 1893.
36 Ibid.
37 Ibid.
38 'The Jew in Ireland', Lyceum, Vol. VI, No. 70 (July 1893), pp. 215–18. Fr Thomas Finlay, the Jesuit social reformer and promoter of the co-operative movement, wrote a series of articles in the Lyceum in 1892–93; in these he did not express his opposition to Jews on grounds of race, religion or nationality but rather on their alleged involvement in moneylending. See Fr Thomas Finlay, 'The Jew Amongst Us', Lyceum, Vol. VI, No. 71, p. 235, which refers to the use of Christian blood in the making of Jewish ceremonial bread; Lyceum, June, July, August/September 1892, Vol. V, Nos. 58, 59, 60, pp. 195, 221 and 256 respectively. See also Thomas Finlay, 'A Model Masonic Government', Vol. VI, No. 67, p. 153. Reference supplied by Fr Brian Murphy, Glenstal Abbey, County Limerick. Fr Tom Morrissey confirms that a copy of the Lyceum in the Jesuit library in Dublin had the name of Fr Finlay written on it.
39 'The Jew in Ireland', pp. 215–16.
40 Ibid., pp. 216–17.
41 Ibid., p. 217.
42 Ibid., pp. 217–18.
43 Ibid., p. 218.
44 Ibid.
45 See Eugen Weber, Action Française: Royalism and Reaction in Twentieth-Century France (Stanford: Stanford University Press, 1962), pp. 1–7.
46 Fear of 'Jewish power' was particularly prevalent in 'Catholic' France at the turn of the century where the radical ministry of E. Combes began on 2 June 1902. On 18 March 1903 many Catholic

religious orders were dissolved. The French ambassador was withdrawn from the Vatican on 17 May 1904, and church and state were separated on 6 December 1905.

47 Quoted by John Hellman, 'The Jews in the "New Middle Ages": Jacques Maritain's Anti-Semitism in its Times', in Robert Royal (ed.), *Jacques Maritain and the Jews* (Indiana: American Maritain Association, 1994), p. 90. See also Eugen Weber, *Action Française*, p. 33.

48 Eugen Weber, *The Nationalist Revival in France, 1905–1914* (Berkeley and Los Angeles: University of California Press, 1968), pp. 1–68.

49 I am cautious about attributing all the anti-Semitic content in the paper to the personal pen of Griffith, but as editor he took overall responsibility for the content of his paper.

50 *United Irishman,* 23 September 1899.

51 *Ibid.*

52 An editorial in *La Croix* stated: 'On every side, people demand a strong man, a man ready to risk his life to wrest France from the traitors, the factious, and the imbeciles who are handing it over to the foreigner … And who will deliver us from this gang of hoodlums.' Eugen Weber, *Action Française*, p. 33.

53 *United Irishman*, 5 August 1899.

54 *Ibid.* Another article, on 19 August, opined that 'two thirds of the foreign journalists, who are not English or Yankee, are Jews'.

55 Jean-Denis Bredin, *The Affair: The Case of Alfred Dreyfus* (New York: George Braziller, 1986), pp. 402–51.

56 *United Irishman*, 16 September 1899.

57 *United Irishman*, 26 August 1899. For background on Frederick Ryan, who was the first national secretary of the Socialist Party of Ireland, see Manus O'Riordan (ed.), *Socialism, Democracy and the Church* (Dublin: Labour History Workshop, 1984), p. 69; Manus O'Riordan (ed.), *Sinn Féin and Reaction, articles by Frederick Ryan with obituaries by Jim Larkin, Arthur Griffith and F. Sheehy Skeffington* (Dublin: Labour History Workshop, 1984), p. 51. I am very grateful to Manus O'Riordan for supplying me with copies of these publications.

58 Chamberlain to Under-Secretary, 23 February 1903, CSORP, 1905/23538, NAI.

59 Irish pawnbrokers, for example, must not have been pleased to face competition from Jewish traders prepared to sell on a weekly credit system to the poorest sectors of society. A bizarre event

took place in summer 1899 which did not endear Jewry to members of the Royal Irish Academy and to Irish archaeologists. British Israelites unsuccessfully excavated the Rath of the Synods at the Hill of Tara in search of the Ark of the Covenant. See G. F. Mitchell, 'Antiquities', in T. Ó Raifeartaigh (ed.), *The Royal Irish Academy: A Bicentennial History 1785–1985* (Dublin: Royal Irish Academy, 1985), p. 151. R. A. S. Macalister, in a paper read to the Royal Irish Academy on 28 January 1919, said that the rath had been 'almost wholly devastated' in the excavation: 'had the Anglo-Israelites even done as much to record what they actually did find we might have partly forgiven them. But they did not even make this small compensation for their offence against science and against reason.' See *Proceedings of the Royal Irish Academy*, Vol. XXXIV, 1917–19, pp. 252–3. For background to this excavation, see the Tara Committee's report in the *Royal Society of Antiquaries of Ireland Journal*, Series 5, Vol. XIII, 1903, pp. 102–4. It concluded: 'the condition in which the Rath of the Synods has been left is deplorable'. For further details, see Seán P. Ó Riordáin, *Tara: The Monument on the Hill* (Dundalk: Dundalgan Press, 1954), p. 22; see also Peter C. Woodman, 'Who Possesses Tara?: Politics in Archaeology in Ireland', in *Theory in Archaeology: A World Perspective* (London: Routledge, 1995), pp. 278–97.

60 Statistical Abstract of Ireland, 1931 (Stationery Office, Dublin, 1931), table 8, p. 5.

61 *Ibid*. The Dublin and Dundalk experiences generally contrasted sharply with changes in the rest of the country.

62 Willie W. Gleeson, 'City of Commerce', *Old Limerick Journal*, No. 11, 1982, p. 25.

63 Pat Feely, 'Servant boys and girls in Co. Limerick', *Old Limerick Journal*, No. 1, 1979, p. 33.

64 *Ibid*., pp. 32–5. A detailed account of the realities of life – in which the working day ran from 4.30a.m. to 9.30p.m. – can be gleaned from Mary Carbery, *The Farm by Lough Gur: the Story of Mary Fogarty* (Sissy O'Brien, Longmans Green & Co.), extracts of which are reproduced in J. Kemmy (ed), *The Limerick Compendium*, (Dublin: Gill and Macmillan, 1997), pp. 76–9.

65 P. J. Ryan, 'Poverty and Pawnshops', *Old Limerick Journal*, No. 7, 1981, p. 10.

66 *Ibid*.

67 *Ibid*.

68 Thomas Morrissey, SJ, *Bishop Edward Thomas O'Dwyer of Limerick* (Dublin: Four Courts, 2003), p. 317ff, offers a good insight into the poverty, degradation and attempts to cope with it in Limerick at this time.

69 Born in Thomondgate on 19 August 1870, Creagh was from a middle-class family. His mother died when he was eight. His father removed him from the Christian Brothers' School to the diocesan seminary where the future bishop of Limerick, Dr Edward Thomas O'Dwyer, was rector. He returned to the Christian Brothers when the school closed. He entered the Redemptorists at the age of fourteen. He studied for three years in the juvenate with the order before going to Liverpool, where he did his novitiate. He then moved to South Devon and was professed on 18 October 1888. He was ordained on 1 September 1895. He spent five years as a professor of scripture and theology in England. He was sent to Belfast and then moved to Esker, Athenry, Co. Galway. From there he was transferred to Limerick. See 'Father Creagh – His voyage to the Philippines', undated press cutting in the Holy Family Chronicles, 1900–42 (Part 1), Redemptorist Archives, Redemptorist House, Limerick (hereafter cited as Holy Family Chronicles, Limerick). See also Creagh's curriculum vitae, written in Liverpool in 1887 while he was in the novitiate. My thanks to Fr Brendan McConvery, archivist, Marianella, Dublin.

70 Interview with Creagh, 'Catholic and Jew, Father Creagh in Belfast, his version of the crusade', *Northern Whig*, 8 February 1904.

71 Samuel J. Boland, 'Fr John Creagh in the Kimberleys', *Old Limerick Journal*, No. 23 (Spring 1988), p. 152. Creagh spent much of his later life in Australia; Boland wrote: 'He embarrassed the [Australian] government by speaking about the grant of one shilling a year to the Sisters' mission ... He enraged the pearling companies by describing, with an abundance of vivid detail, the exploitation of crews and divers, most of them Asiatics, living for years in exile to support impoverished families.'

72 Creagh declared his fear about undertaking his new position, but trusted in the goodness of God to help him to continue the splendid work of the arch-confraternity. Undated press cuttings in Holy Family Chronicles, Limerick.

73 *Ibid*.

74 Early that year on 6 January 1904 Creagh's stepmother died and

he officiated at the funeral. Her remains were removed from St Munchin's Church the following day and taken by rail to Miltown Malbay, Co. Clare, where she was buried at Killarin cemetary. See *Limerick Leader*, 7 January 1904, quoted in Des Ryan, 'The Jews of Limerick' (Part 2), *Old Limerick Journal*, No. 18 (Winter 1985), p. 36.

75 Cutting from the *Limerick Journal*, 13 January 1904 in Holy Family Chronicles, Limerick.

76 This sermon was delivered again the following night. It may even have been given on the Wednesday evening.

77 A letter from 'a Limerick Confraternity man', dated 20 January 1904, attacked Davitt for his defence of Jews: 'Limerickmen love their native land, and its grand traditions, many of which are immortalised in song and story, but which we well know would not improve by affinity with aliens to our Faith and Fatherland, aye, not only aliens but avowed enemies. One tradition I would especially draw attention to as sung by Tom Moore, viz. – "Rich and rare were the gems she wore" – as testifying to the purity of the Irish character. How many such are to be found in the mishna? Or I wonder how long would those precious gems remain unsullied in the midst of a Jewish population. This strikes me all the more forcefully, as while I write a matter comes to hand which informs me that an old Jew – grey and decrepid – standing in his doorway a few evenings ago, invites into his parlour some young women passing by, offering as a gift a new dress. One came on who no sooner heard the invitation than like a true daughter of Limerick hurled the old wretch from his battlement with the same weapons as of yore.' Davitt was also attacked in the letters columns of the *Limerick Echo* and the *Munster News* but he was defended in the *London Times* on 23 January 1904. See also Hyman, *The Jews of Ireland*, p. 216 and Shillman, *A Short History of the Jews*, p. 137. For a brief description of Davitt's views on the persecution of the Jews, see T. W. Moody, *Davitt and Irish Revolution 1848–82* (Oxford: Clarendon Press, 1982).

78 Holy Family Chronicles, Limerick.

79 Ryan, 'The Jews of Limerick', p. 37.

80 See 'A Limerick priest's attack on the Jews', *Jewish Chronicle*, 22 January 1904 (quoted in Ryan, 'The Jews of Limerick', p. 37).

81 Cutting from *Jewish Chronicle*, 22 January 1904, Holy Family Chronicles, Limerick; the article is date-lined 17 January, but there can be little doubt that it was sent on the evening of the

18th after the intimidation and the threats of violence, and in fact the report refers to 'today' as Monday.

82 'Mischief-making in Limerick', *Jewish Chronicle*, 22 January 1904.

83 Among those who criticised Creagh were I. Julian Grande, director of the Irish Mission to Jews. At a meeting in Dublin he said he was sorry to find that a strong feeling of anti-Semitism had made itself felt in Limerick. A resolution was unanimously passed condemning the unjust and unchristian attacks made on the Jewish community in Limerick (undated cutting from the *Limerick Journal*, probably 19 January 1904, in Holy Family Chronicles, Limerick

84 Ryan 'The Jews of Limerick', p. 37

85 On this issue Creagh based his arguments on a very uncritical reading of the anti-Semitic work of l'Abbé René F. Rohrbacher, *Histoire Universelle de l'Eglise Catholique*, 5 vols (no publisher, 1842). The later edition of 1856 has 29 volumes. Both editions are in the Library of Congress, Washington DC. See also reference in press cutting, *Holy Family Chronicles*, Limerick.

86 O'Hara report, 19 January 1904, CSORP, 1905/23538, NAI.

87 Considine minute, 19 January 1904, CSORP, 1905/23538, NAI.

88 Considine minute, 21 January 1904, CSORP, 1905/23538, NAI.

89 Hayes report, 20 January 1904, CSORP, 1905/23538, NAI.

90 O'Hara report, 22 January 1904, CSORP, 1905/23538, NAI.

91 Undated cutting from the *Limerick Journal* in Holy Family Chronicles, Limerick.

92 Ryan, 'The Jews of Limerick', p. 37.

93 A file marked 'Jews' containing two letters from David Alexander, president of the London Committee of Deputies of British Jews, is what remains in the archives. See File 35, Edward Thomas O'Dwyer papers, Limerick Diocesan Archives. I am grateful to Bishop Donal Murray for giving me access to the O'Dwyer papers.

94 The Redemptorist Holy Family Chronicle is not particularly helpful in this regard while the Domestic Chronicle merely recorded the following at the time: Rev. J. Creagh denounced the Jews of Limerick at the Confraternity meeting for their extortions. Mr Davitt replied by an angry and abusive letter in the *Freeman's Journal*. At the next meeting the men clapped their hands when Fr Creagh appeared in the pulpit. A meeting was held to protest against Davitt's letter and letters were published in the city newspapers attacking him. Assaults were made in some

places on the Jews, and some of those who did so were fined heavily by the Magistrates (Mt St Alphonsus, Domestic Chronicle, Vol. 3, 1899–1911, Redemptorist Archives, Redemptorist House, Limerick.

95 Two-page excerpt entitled 'An Extract from the Provincial Chronicles 1904', in Holy Family Chronicles, Limerick. It began: Fr Creagh preached many sermons to the Confraternity at Limerick on the Jews; showing how extortionate they were: giving details of their evil deeds in every country in Europe from the earliest times. Soon afterwards the Jews were assaulted in the streets and Jewish families were reduced to such distress that they had to leave Limerick. The Jews were doing great harm by their extortions and the sale of immoral pictures. However their defence was taken up by the Protestants of Limerick and violent attacks were made on Fr Creagh. Some English newspapers published most violent attacks both on Fr Creagh and the Catholics of Limerick. 'The Times' had leading articles on the subject in which they defended the Jews and attacked the Catholic Church. At the Protestant Synod of Bishops in Dublin Dr Bunbury the Protestant Bishop of Limerick spoke strongly against Fr Creagh and expressed his astonishment that he was not silenced by his Superiors. He was called a pulpit firebrand and an ecclesiastical incendery [sic].'

96 Ibid.

97 This is speculation on my part, but it would appear that O'Dwyer was angry at having his diocese a centre of anti-Semitic outbursts which would be an indirect criticism of his handling of affairs.

98 Two-page excerpt entitled 'an Extract from the Provincial Chronicles 1904', in Holy Family Chronicles, Limerick.

99 Alexander to Logue, 8 April 1904, File 35, Edward Thomas O'Dwyer papers, Limerick Diocesan Archives.

100 Alexander to O'Dwyer, 25 April 1904 (enclosing a copy of his letter to Logue), File 35, Edward Thomas O'Dwyer papers, Limerick Diocesan Archives.

101 Fr Brendan McConvery to Dermot Keogh, 3 May 1997. Fr McConvery, who has written on the history of the Redemptorists in Ireland, gave me generous assistance in the writing of this chapter. He recounts a saying among Redemptorists of an earlier generation about the three superior generals whose rule spanned the late nineteenth and early twentieth centuries: 'Mauron was all head, Raus was all heart, Murray was neither head nor heart.'

102 Mt St Alphonsus, Domestic Chronicle, Vol. 3 (1899–1911), Redemptorist Archives, Redemptorist House, Limerick.

103 *Ibid.*

104 Address to Raus by the Hebrew Congregation of Limerick, Synagogue Chambers, 63 Coloney Street. Original kept in Holy Family Chronicles, Limerick.

105 Two-page excerpt entitled 'an Extract from the Provincial Chronicles 1904', in Holy Family Chronicles, Limerick.

106 Letter from P. Hayes, secretary of the Mechanics' Institute, Bank Place, 22 January 1904, in Holy Family Chronicles, Limerick.

107 Undated press cutting in Holy Family Chronicles, Limerick.

108 See *Northern Whig*, 8 February 1904, republished in the *Limerick Leader*, 17 February 1904 and quoted in Ryan, 'The Jews of Limerick', p. 38.

109 *Ibid.* The same interview was the subject of an editorial in the *Derry Journal*, 12 February 1904.

110 Holy Family Chronicles, Limerick.

111 Two-page excerpt entitled 'an Extract from the Provincial Chronicles 1904', in Holy Family Chronicles, Limerick.

112 Cutting from the *London Times* and from the *Cork Examiner*, 6 April 1904, in Holy Family Chronicles, Limerick.

113 *United Irishman*, 23 April 1904.

114 *Ibid.*

115 *Ibid.*

116 *Ibid.*

117 *Ibid.*

118 Cutting in Holy Family Chronicles, Limerick. Jaffe went on to explain an incident which occurred in Killaloe, Co. Clare, about six or seven years before. A missioner gave such a fiery sermon on the crucifixion that the following day Jews who had come to the town to trade were shunned like lepers and in other cases beset by a wild and infuriated mob. Jaffe sent a letter to the local bishop and that had the effect of restoring peace.

119 Church of Ireland clergyman E. H. Lewis-Crosby had a critical letter in the *London Times* on 11 April 1904. There were further critical reports in the *Irish Times*, 13 April 1904 and in the *Northern Mail*, 15 April 1904. The *London Times*, carrying many letters critical of the priest in its correspondence columns, condemned the attacks on the Limerick Jews in an editorial on 5 April. An article in the *Birmingham Post* of 15 March 1904 was

critical of the outbreak of intolerance and intimidation in Limerick.

120 Ryan, 'The Jews of Limerick', p. 38.

121 County Inspector Thomas Hayes to Dublin Castle, 28 January
1904, CSORP, 1905/23538, NAI. Emphasis in quote added by
Dublin Castle.

122 List of allegations investigated by the police, January–March
1904, CSORP, 1905/23538, NAI.

123 *Ibid.*

124 *Ibid.*

125 *Ibid.*

126 *Ibid.*

127 Considine minute, 8 April 1904, CSORP, 1905/23538, NAI.

128 Dublin Castle minute, 9 April 1904, CSORP 1905/23538, NAI

129 Considine minute, 9 April 1904, CSORP, 1905/23538, NAI.

130 O'Hara report, 7 April 1904, CSORP, 1905/23538, NAI.

131 Considine minute, 14 April 1904, CSORP, 1905/23538, NAI.

132 O'Hara report, 14 May 1904, CSORP, 1905/23538, NAI.

133 *Irish Times*, 16 April 1904.

134 *Ibid.*

135 *Ibid.*

136 *Ibid.*

137 *Ibid.*

138 *Freeman's Journal*, 16 April 1904.

139 O'Hara report, 22 April 1904, CSORP, 1905/23538, NAI.

140 'The Jewish question – action of the corporation', *Limerick
Chronicle*, 21 April 1904.

141 *Ibid.*

142 Contrary to the concluding statement of the editorial (see
document 46), objection had been raised to proselytism in the
past. The relationship between Protestants and Catholics lies
outside the scope of this study but for instance a man named Dr
John Long was a controversial figure. In Limerick since 1897, he
ran a free medical clinic. He suffered intimidation from those who
objected to his attempts to make converts to Protestantism. Reference to his activities may be found in Ryan, 'The Jews of Limerick', p. 38. See also Anon. (An Irishman), *Intolerance in Ireland
– Facts not Fiction* (London: Simpkin Marshall, Hamilton, Kent
and Co., 1913), pp. 36–49.

143 William J. Moloney, 'The libel of Limerick', *Leader*, 30 April
1904, p. 148.

144 *Ibid.*
145 William J. Moloney, 'Limerick and the Jews', *Leader*, 7 May 1904, p. 71.
146 William J. Moloney, 'The libel of Limerick', *Leader*, 30 April 1904, p. 150.
147 Hyman, *The Jews of Ireland*, pp. 216-17.
148 Ryan, 'The Jews of Limerick', p. 39.
149 Dublin Castle minute, 6 October 1904, CSORP, 1905/23538, NAI.
150 Hayes report, 12 March 1905, CSORP, 1905/23538, NAI.
151 Dublin Castle report, 13 March 1905, CSORP, 1905/23538, NAI.
152 *Ibid.* District Inspector O'Hara had filed a very detailed report on this topic on 12 March 1905. Of the total of 49 who had left, 16 were men, 8 were women and there were 25 children. The three families who left for private reasons were that of 'Rabbi Goldberg' (possibly a reference to Louis Goldberg, who was not a rabbi but who did have a synagogue in his house during the split), who left owing to the settlement of 'an inter-Jewish schism during the prevalence of which two Rabbis were employed in Limerick', and two families called Weinronk who left to join the heads of that family in South Africa. Of the 26 families that remained, 18 were in 'poor circumstances'. Their trade in the city as pedlars and traders was 'gone' and not likely to return. O'Hara said that the statement that the Jews were left severely alone was true in general, but people still dealt with a dentist called Jaffe and a furniture dealer called Toohey.
153 Cutting from House of Commons debate, 4 July 1905, CSORP, 1905/23538, NAI.
154 Levin to Long, 11 July 1905, CSORP, 1905/23538, NAI.
155 Hyman, *The Jews of Ireland*, p. 217.
156 See copy of article by Asher Benson, 'Storm before the Storm', about the divisions within the Jewish community in Limerick over the purchase of a Jewish burial ground. There is also correspondence between Benson and one of Levin's sons, Salmond, in Box 39, Irish Jewish Museum Archives, Dublin.
157 O'Hara report, 12 March 1905, CSORP, 1905/23538, NAI.
158 See press cutting circa November 1905, Holy Family Chronicles, Limerick. As director of the arch-confraternity, he was also expected to play a role as mediator in trade disputes. On 19 March 1906, for example, he received the text of a resolution

from the secretary of the Mechanics' Institute, J. Hayes, thanking him for 'the noble and businesslike way he brought to a close the protracted dispute in the mason trade.'

159 'A loss to Limerick', editorial in *Limerick Echo*, 24 April 1906.

160 Undated and unidentified cutting in Holy Family Chronicles, Limerick.

161 'Father Creagh's departure', editorial in *Limerick Leader*, 27 April 1906.

162 'Rev. Father Creagh', editorial in *Munster News*, 9 May 1906.

163 *Ibid.*

164 Undated and unidentified cutting in Holy Family Chronicles, Limerick.

165 *Ibid.*

166 *Ibid.*

167 After the Philippines, Creagh worked in Northern Australia and in New Zealand, all the time in the service of poorer sections of those societies. Wherever he went, controversy dogged him. In any future study, it would be worth attempting to place Creagh in his wider intellectual and cultural context by examining his family background, his formation in the seminary, the ethos of the Redemptorist order at the time, the links through his order with French Catholicism, the place of the order in the contemporary debate on anti-Semitism, and the nature and structure of Limerick society at the turn of the century. This wider study may reveal Creagh to be at once villain and victim – the prey of the intellectual anti-Semitism of his church and of his time.

168 Interview with Richard Haslam, Cork, November, 1997.

169 *Ibid.*

170 Information kindly supplied by Denis Leonard, Limerick Civic Trust.

171 See invitation card, Limerick Civic Trust archives, Limerick.

172 *Irish Times*, 15 November 1990; *Limerick Leader*, 17 November 1990.

173 *Limerick Leader*, 17 November 1990.

174 *Irish Times*, 15 November 1990.

CENSUS OF IRELAND 1901

26 Bowman St.

NAME	RELATION	RELIGION	EDUCATION	AGE	SEX	OCCUPATION	MARRIED	BORN
Solomon Aronovitch	Husband	Hebrew	R/W	29	M	Draper Pedlar	Married	Russia
Sarah Aronovitch	Wife	Hebrew	R/W	30	F	—	Married	Russia
Edith Aronovitch	Daughter	Hebrew	—	6	F	—	not Married	Limerick
Isack Aronovitch	Son	Hebrew	—	2	M	—	not Married	Limerick

40 Henry St.

NAME	RELATION	RELIGION	EDUCATION	AGE	SEX	OCCUPATION	MARRIED	BORN
Marcus J. Blonde	Husband	Jewish	R/W	38	M	Draper & Grocer	Married	Russia
Esther B. Blonde	Wife	Jewish	—	35	F	—	Married	Russia
Gertrude Blonde	Daughter	Jewish	—	11	F	Scholar	not Married	Limerick City
Rosie Blonde	Daughter	Jewish	—	7	F	—	not Married	Limerick City
Lily Blonde	Daughter	Jewish	—	5	F	—	not Married	Limerick City
Harold Blonde	Son	Jewish	cannot read	4	M	—	not Married	Limerick City
Moses Greenfield	Boarder	Jewish	cannot read	72	M	—	Widower	Russia
Katie Hartigan	Servant	R/C	cannot read	16	F	General Servant	not Married	Limerick City

CENSUS OF IRELAND 1901

40 Henry St.

NAME	RELATION	RELIGION	EDUCATION	AGE	SEX	OCCUPATION	MARRIED	BORN
Jacob Barron	Husband	Jewish	R/W	49	M	Draper	Married	Russia
Rachel Barron	Wife	Jewish	R/W	45	F	—	Married	Russia
Myer? Barron	Son	Jewish	R/W	19	M	Drapery business Traveller	not Married	Russia
Abraham Barron	Son	Jewish	R/W	17	M	Watch Maker Finisher	not Married	Limerick City
David Barron	Son	Jewish	R/W	14	M	—	not Married	Limerick City
Lorrie Barron	Son	Jewish	R/W	13	M	Scholar	not Married	Limerick City
Sarah Barron	Daughter	Jewish	R/W	16	F	Scholar	not Married	—
Leah Barron	Daughter	Jewish	R/W	6	F	Scholar	not Married	Limerick City

79 Colooney St.

NAME	RELATION	RELIGION	EDUCATION	AGE	SEX	OCCUPATION	MARRIED	BORN
David Crapman	Husband	Jewish	Cannot read	72	M	General Draper	Married	Russia
Ruth Crapman	Wife	Jewish	Cannot read	50	F	—	Married	Russia
Hyman S. Crapman	Son	Jewish	Read only	28	M	Draper Pedlar	Married	Russia
Ethel Crapman	Daughter-in-law	Jewish	Cannot read	21	F	House Keeper	Married	Russia
Eva Crapman	Granddaughter	Jewish	Cannot read	9?	F	None	—	Limerick City

CENSUS OF IRELAND 1901

11 Emmet Place

NAME	RELATION	RELIGION	EDUCATION	AGE	SEX	OCCUPATION	MARRIED	BORN
Ephraim Farher	Husband	Hebrew/W	R/W	41	M	Draper Pedlar	Married	Russia
Rachel Farher	Wife	Hebrew/W	R/W	40	F	—	Married	Russia
Florrie Farher	Daughter	Hebrew/W	R/W	16	F	Scholar	not Married	Russia
Rebecca Farher	Daughter	Hebrew/W	R/W	9	F	Scholar	—	Limerick City
Joseph Farher	Son	Hebrew/W	R/W	7	M	Scholar	—	Limerick City
Bernard Farher	Son	Hebrew/W	C/R	6	M	Scholar	—	Limerick City
Jacob Lentin	Boarder	Hebrew/W	R/W	20	M	Draper Pedlar	—	Russia

82 Colooney St. (Shop)

NAME	RELATION	RELIGION	EDUCATION	AGE	SEX	OCCUPATION	MARRIED	BORN
Barnet Gould	Husband	Jewish	R/W	29	M	Grocer	Married	Russia
Eide? Gould	Wife	Jewish	Do	27	F	—	Married	Russia
Sarah Gould	Daughter	Jewish	—	4	F	None	not Married	Limerick
Bernard Gould	Son	Jewish	—	2	M	do	do	Limerick
Elley O'Donnell	Servant	R/C	R/W	14	F	General Domestic Servant	do	Limerick

CENSUS OF IRELAND 1901

23 Colooney St.

NAME	RELATION	RELIGION	EDUCATION	AGE	SEX	OCCUPATION	MARRIED	BORN
Barnet Graff	Husband	Hebrew	R/W	26	M	Drapery Shopkeeper	Married	Russia
Sarah Graff	Wife	Hebrew	R/W	25	F	—	Married	Russia
Fanny Graff	Daughter	Hebrew	cannot read	2	F	None	not Married	Limerick City

77 Colooney St.

NAME	RELATION	RELIGION	EDUCATION	AGE	SEX	OCCUPATION	MARRIED	BORN
Hyman Graff	Husband	Hebrew	R/W	30	M	Draper Pedlar	Married	Russia
Florey Graff	Wife	Hebrew	read only	28	F	—	Married	Russia
Dora Graff	Daughter	Hebrew	R/W	9	F	Scholar	not Married	Limerick
Sarah Graff	Daughter	Hebrew	R/W	7	F	Scholar	not Married	Limerick
Isaac Aronow?	Nephew	Hebrew	R/W	19	M	Pedlar	not Married	Russia
Elley Reilly	Servant	R/C	R/W	21	F	General Domestic Servant	not Married	Co. Cork

CENSUS OF IRELAND 1901

47 Henry St.

NAME	RELATION	RELIGION	EDUCATION	AGE	SEX	OCCUPATION	MARRIED	BORN
Louis Goldberg	Husband	Hebrew	R/W	31	M.	Wholesale Draper	Married	Russia
Rachel Goldberg	Wife	Hebrew	R/W	27	F	—	Married	Russia
Fanny Goldberg	Daughter	Hebrew	R/W	7	F	Scholar	not Married	Limerick City
Molly Goldberg	Daughter	Hebrew	R/W	5	F	Scholar	not Married	Limerick City
Henry Goldberg	Son	Hebrew	cannot read	2	M	—	not Married	Limerick City
Elie Goldberg	Mother	Hebrew	cannot read	63	F	—	Widow	Russia
Joseph Sandler	Brother-in-Law	Hebrew	R/W	19	F	Servant Domestic	not Married	Limerick City
Mary Ann Morrissey	Servant	R/C	R/W	19	F	Servant Domestic	not Married	Limerick City

15 Emmet Place

NAME	RELATION	RELIGION	EDUCATION	AGE	SEX	OCCUPATION	MARRIED	BORN
Samuel Goldberg	Husband	Jewish	R/W	27.5	M	Pedlar Draper	Married	Poland
Rachel Goldberg	Wife	Jewish	do	22.0	F	—	Married	Poland
Simon Goldberg	Son	Jewish	do	7.0	M	Scholar	Married	Poland
Harry Goldberg	Son	Jewish	do	5.3	M	Scholar	not Married	Limerick
Sarah Goldberg	Daughter	Jewish	do	4.6	F	Scholar	not Married	Limerick
Hannah Goldberg	Daughter	Jewish	do	1.1	F	—	not Married	Limerick

CENSUS OF IRELAND 1901

9 Colooney St.

NAME	RELATION	RELIGION	EDUCATION	AGE	SEX	OCCUPATION	MARRIED	BORN
Bernard Goldberg	Husband	Hebrew	R/W	41	M	Draper Pedlar	Married	Russia
Sima Goldberg	Wife	Hebrew	cannot read	35	F	—	Married	Russia
Edith Goldberg	Daughter	Hebrew	R/W	15	F	None	not Married	Russia
Harry Goldberg	Son	Hebrew	R/W	14	M	Draper Pedlar	not Married	Russia
Benny Goldberg	Son	Hebrew	R/W	9	M	Scholar	not Married	Limerick
Rebecca Goldberg	Daughter	Hebrew	R/W	6	F	Scholar	not Married	Limerick
Isack Goldberg	Son	Hebrew	R/W	4	M	Scholar	not Married	Limerick
Sarah Goldberg	Daughter	Hebrew	cannot read	3	F	None	not Married	Limerick

7 Newenham St.

NAME	RELATION	RELIGION	EDUCATION	AGE	SEX	OCCUPATION	MARRIED	BORN
Solomon Ginsberg	Husband	Jew Hebrew	R/W	42	M	Draper Business	Married	Russia
							Nationalised 1893 in England	
Fanny Ginsberg	Wife	Jew Hebrew	R/W	40	F		Married	Russia
Rebecca Ginsberg	Daughter	Jew Hebrew	R/W	16	F	School children	not Married	Limerick
Alick Ginsberg	Son	Jew Hebrew	R/W	14	M	Scholar	not Married	Limerick
Rosie Ginsberg	Daughter	Jew Hebrew	R/W	12	F	Scholar	not Married	Limerick
Jacob Ginsberg	Son	Jew Hebrew	R/W	10	M	Scholar	not Married	Limerick
Annie Ginsberg	Daughter	Jew Hebrew	R/W	9	F	Scholar	not Married	Limerick
Isaac Ginsberg	Son	Jew Hebrew	R/W	8	M	Scholar	not Married	Limerick
Raphael Ginsberg	Son	Jew Hebrew	R/W	6	M	Scholar	not Married	Limerick
Katie O'Brien	Servant	R/C	R/W	21	F	General Domestic Servant	not Married	Clogheen, Co. Tipperary
Isaac Lenthum	Boarder	Hebrew	R/W	22		Draper Business	not Married	Russia

CENSUS OF IRELAND 1901

19 Colooney St.

NAME	RELATION	RELIGION	EDUCATION	AGE	SEX	OCCUPATION	MARRIED	BORN
Solomon Jerome	Husband	Hebrew	R/W	28	M	Pedlar	Married	Russia
Hannah Jerome	Wife	Hebrew	R/W	27	F	—	Married	Russia
Anna Jerome	Daughter	Hebrew	R/W	3	F	None	not Married	Limerick
Leser Jerome	Daughter	Hebrew	R/W	10	M	None	not Married	Limerick
Charles Berman	Boarder	Hebrew	R/W	23	M	Travels Howken	not Married	Russia
Mary Corbett	Servant	R/C	R/W	19	F	General Domestic Servant		Limerick

64 Colooney St.

NAME	RELATION	RELIGION	EDUCATION	AGE	SEX	OCCUPATION	MARRIED	BORN
Benjamin Jaffey	Husband	Hebrew	R/W	48	M	Pedlar	Married	Russia
Rachel Jaffey	Wife	Hebrew	R/W	47	F	—	Married	Russia
Sydney A. Jaffey	Son	Hebrew	R/W	22	M	Dentist Cork Queens Cork	—	Russia
Edith Jaffey	Daughter	Hebrew	R/W	20	F	—	—	Russia
Alice Galligan	Servant	R/C	R/W	22	F	—	—	Ireland

CENSUS OF IRELAND 1901

31 Colooney St.

NAME	RELATION	RELIGION	EDUCATION	AGE	SEX	OCCUPATION	MARRIED	BORN
Marcus L. Jaffe	Husband	Hebrew	R/W	26	M	Dental Mechanic	Married	Russia
Leagh Jaffe	Wife	Hebrew	—	25	F	—	Married	Russia
Henry Jaffe	Son	Hebrew	No	3	M	—	—	Ireland
Rose Jaffe	Daughter	Hebrew	No	42 mts	F	—	—	Ireland
Norah Ryan	Servant	R/C	R/N	21	F	Servant	—	Ireland

25 Bowman St.

NAME	RELATION	RELIGION	EDUCATION	AGE	SEX	OCCUPATION	MARRIED	BORN
Solomon Kramer	Husband	Hebrew	R/W	32	M	Shop Manager & Pedlar	Married	Russia
Miram? Kramer	Wife	Hebrew	R/W	27	F	—	Married	Russia
Samy Kramer	Son	Hebrew	R/W	6	M	Scholar	not Married	Limerick City
Rosie Kramer	Daughter	Hebrew	C/R	5	F	—	not Married	Limerick City
Isidore Kramer	Son	Hebrew	C/R	3	M	—	not Married	Limerick City
Moses? Kramer	Son	Hebrew	C/R	1	M	—	not Married	Limerick City

(2 Jewish families living at this address)

(Kramers & Shenkmans?)

CENSUS OF IRELAND 1901

87 Colooney St. (Shop)

NAME	RELATION	RELIGION	EDUCATION	AGE	SEX	OCCUPATION	MARRIED	BORN
Moses Keane	Husband	Jew	No	60	M	Shop keeper	Married	Russia
Minnie Keane	Wife	Jewess	None	40	F	—	Married	Russia

18 Colooney St.

NAME	RELATION	RELIGION	EDUCATION	AGE	SEX	OCCUPATION	MARRIED	BORN
Elias B. Levin	Husband	Jewish	Read and Write	36	M	Jewish Minister	Married	Russia
Annie Levin	Wife	Jewish	cannot read	33	F	—	Married	Russia
Harry Levin	Son	Jewish	R/W	16	M	Scholar	not Married	Limerick
Edith Levin	Daughter	Jewish	R/W	14	F	Scholar	not Married	Limerick
Sarah Levin	Daughter	Jewish	R/W	10	F	Scholar	not Married	Limerick
Isaac L. Levin	Son	Jewish	R/W	9	M	Scholar	not Married	Limerick
Samuel W. Levin	Son	Jewish	—	7	M	Scholar	not Married	America
Michael Levin	Son	Jewish	cannot read	5	M	Scholar	not Married	Limerick
Annie Levin	Daughter	Jewish	cannot read	3	F	None	not Married	Limerick
Bella Levin	Daughter	Jewish	cannot read	11	F	None	not Married	Limerick
Jane Meade	Servant	RC	R/W	22	F	Domestic Servant	not Married	Limerick

CENSUS OF IRELAND 1901

26 Richmond St.

NAME	RELATION	RELIGION	EDUCATION	AGE	SEX	OCCUPATION	MARRIED	BORN
Julian Martinson	Husband	Hebrew	R/W	30	M	Draper Dealer	Married	Russia
Annie Martinson	Wife	Hebrew	R/W	22	F	—	Married	Russia
Abraham Martinson	Son	Hebrew	—	8	M	—	Single	Limerick City
Sarah Martinson	Daughter	Hebrew	—	6	F	—	Single	Limerick City
Kate Ahern	Servant	R/C	R/W	18	F	Domestic Servant	Single	Limerick City

24 Colooney St.

NAME	RELATION	RELIGION	EDUCATION	AGE	SEX	OCCUPATION	MARRIED	BORN
Woulfe Maissell	Husband	Hebrew	R/W	55	M	Pedlar	Married	Russia
July? Maissell	Wife	Hebrew	—	54	F	—	Married	Russia
Maurice Maissell	Son	Hebrew	R/W	24	M	Pedlar	Married	Russia
Florrie Maissell	Daughter	Hebrew	R/W	17	F	—	—	Russia
Julius Greene	Nephew	Hebrew	R/W	20	M	Pedlar	—	Russia

CENSUS OF IRELAND 1901

63 Colooney St. (Synagogue)

NAME	RELATION	RELIGION	EDUCATION	AGE	SEX	OCCUPATION	MARRIED	BORN
Jacob Newman	Husband	Hebrew	R/W	48	M	Draper Pedlar	Married	Russia
Sarah Newman	Wife	Hebrew	—	35	F	—	Married	—
Wolf Newman	Son	Hebrew	R/W	18	M	Clerk Pedlar	—	—
Fanny Newman	Daughter	Hebrew	R/W	17	F	—	—	—
Hannah Newman	Daughter	Hebrew	R/W	9	F	—	—	—

5 McNamara Place/Tce

NAME	RELATION	RELIGION	EDUCATION	AGE	SEX	OCCUPATION	MARRIED	BORN
Samuel Racussen	Husband	Jew	C/R	30	M	Draper Pedlar	Married	Russia
Esther Racussen	Wife	Jewess	C/R	25	F	—	Married	Russia
Molly Racussen	Daughter	Jewess	C/R	7	F	—	not Married	Limerick
Hilda Racussen	Daughter	Jewess	Read	5	F	Scholar	not Married	Limerick
Mars? Racussen	Son	Jew	—	3	M	Scholar	not Married	Limerick
Lily Racussen	Daughter	Jewess	—	1	F	—	not Married	Limerick

CENSUS OF IRELAND 1901

81 Colooney St.

NAME	RELATION	RELIGION	EDUCATION	AGE	SEX	OCCUPATION	MARRIED	BORN
Isaac Rosenthal	Husband	Jew	—	35	M	Pedlar	Married	Russia
Annie Rosenthal	Wife	Jewess	R/W	22	F	—	Married	Russia
Harry Rosenthal	Son	Jew	—	7	M	Scholar	not Married	Cork
Rebbecca Rosenthal	Daughter	Jewess	—	5	F	School Girl	not Married	America
Hannah Rosenthal	Daughter	Jewess	—	1	F	—	not Married	Limerick

13 Colooney St.

NAME	RELATION	RELIGION	EDUCATION	AGE	SEX	OCCUPATION	MARRIED	BORN
Louis Sieve	Husband	Israelites	R/W	53	M	Draper Pedlar	Married	Russia
Johanna Sieve	Wife	Israelites	R/W	48	F	Draper Pedlar	Married	Russia
Leah Sieve	Daughter	Israelites	R/W	20	F	Draper Pedlar	not Married	Russia
Myer Sieve	Son	Israelites	R/W	16	M	Draper Pedlar	not Married	Limerick
Bella Sieve	Daughter	Israelites	R/W	15	F	Scholar	not Married	Limerick
Michael Sieve	Son	Israelites	R/W	12	M	Scholar	not Married	Limerick
Jacob Sieve	Son	Israelites	R/W	10	M	Scholar	not Married	Limerick
Gerty Baun	Grandchild	Israelites	R/W	6	F	Scholar	not Married	Limerick
David Goldston	Boarder	Israelites	R/W	35	M	Draper Pedlar	Married	Russia

CENSUS OF IRELAND 1901

10 Boherbuoy

NAME	RELATION	RELIGION	EDUCATION	AGE	SEX	OCCUPATION	MARRIED	BORN
Barnett Sochat	Husband	Israelite	R/N	26	M	Draper	Married	Russia
Polly Sochat	Wife	Israelite	R/N	23	F	—	Married	Russia
Simon Sochat	Son	Israelite	C/R	9	M	—	—	Limerick
Nora Curtin	Servant	R/C	R/W	41	F	Servant Domestic	Single	Co. Clare

27 Colooney St.

NAME	RELATION	RELIGION	EDUCATION	AGE	SEX	OCCUPATION	MARRIED	BORN
Mayer William Stein	Husband	Hebrew	R/W	33	M	Dental Mechanic	Married	Russia
Bertha Stein	Wife	Hebrew	R/W	27	F	—	Married	Russia
Mayer? Stein	Son	Hebrew	R/W	6	M	—	—	Limerick
Isaac Stein	Son	Hebrew	R/W	4	M	—	—	Limerick
Mabel? Stein	Daughter	Hebrew	—	4	F	—	—	Limerick
Lena? O'Halloran	Servant	R/C	R/W	18	F	—	—	Co. Clare

CENSUS OF IRELAND 1901

25 Bowman St.

NAME	RELATION	RELIGION	EDUCATION	AGE	SEX	OCCUPATION	MARRIED	BORN
Soloman Shenkman	Husband	Jew	R/W	31	M	Draper Pedlar	Married	Russia
Pollie Shenkman	Wife	Jewess	R/W	23	F	Housekeeper	Married	Russia

(2 Jewish families living at this address: Kramers & Shenkmans)

74 Colooney St.

NAME	RELATION	RELIGION	EDUCATION	AGE	SEX	OCCUPATION	MARRIED	BORN
Wolf Toohey	Husband	Jewish	cannot read	50	M	Pedlar	Married	Russia
Miney Toohey	Wife	Jewish	cannot read	48	F	—	Married	Russia
Philip Toohey	Son	Jewish	R/W	22	M	Draper Pedlar	—	Russia
Fanney Toohey	Daughter	Jewish	R/W	16	F	Scholar	—	Russia
Dora Toohey	Daughter	Jewish	R/W	12	F	Scholar	—	Russia
D. Lewish Clein	Boarder	Jewish		23	M	Draper Pedlar	—	Russia
Lewish Tirademm?	Nephew	Jewish		16	M	Draper Pedlar	—	Russia
Katie Ryan	Servant	R/C		24	F	Domestic Servant	—	Co. Limerick

CENSUS OF IRELAND 1901

72 Colooney St. (Synagogue)

NAME	RELATION	RELIGION	EDUCATION	AGE	SEX	OCCUPATION	MARRIED	BORN
Moses Velitzkin	Husband	Hebrew	R/W	47	M	Jewish Minister	Married	Russia
Judas Velitzkin	Wife	Hebrew	R/W	45	F	—	Married	Russia
Sofia Velitzkin	Daughter	Hebrew	R/W	18	F	Dressmaker	—	Russia
Annie Velitzkin	Daughter	Hebrew	R/W	14	F	—	—	Russia
Sarah Velitzkin	Daughter	Hebrew	R/W	9	F	—	—	Russia

46 Colooney St.

NAME	RELATION	RELIGION	EDUCATION	AGE	SEX	OCCUPATION	MARRIED	BORN
David Weinronk	Husband	Hebrew	R/W	60	M	Drapery Healer	Married	Russia
Sophia Weinronk	Wife	Hebrew	—	58	F	—	Married	Russia
Hanna Weinronk	Daughter	Hebrew	R/W	20	F	—	—	Russia
Simon Weinronk	Son	Hebrew	R/W	18	M	Drapery Dealer	—	Russia
— Kenny	Assistant	R/C	R/W	23	M	General Labour	—	Ireland

27 Bowman St.

NAME	RELATION	RELIGION	EDUCATION	AGE	SEX	OCCUPATION	MARRIED	BORN
Bernard Weinronk	Husband	Hebrew	R/W	30	M	Draper Pedlar	Married	Russia
Sarah Weinronk	Wife	Hebrew	R/W	24	F	—	Married	Russia
Jennette Weinronk	Daughter	Hebrew	C/R	1	F	—	—	Limerick

the limerick boycott   161

Index of Names